American Values

Understanding and Measuring Core Political Values

Laurence O'Rourke, Ph.D.

Copyright © 2019 by Laurence O'Rourke
All Rights Reserved

Published by Barker Pond Press
Acton, Massachusetts

Preface

This book focuses on the measurement of three values that scholars consider critical values in American political culture. My research employed in-depth interviews to explore how individuals think about the values of limited government, moral traditionalism and equality. The research used the battery of values questions in the National Election Studies (NES) as a starting point. The NES survey, funded by the National Science Foundation, has asked a battery of questions related to values for decades, providing a comprehensive time series measurement of the values of the electorate in the United States. The research described in this book advances the study of public opinion by systematically evaluating the sources of instability in the measurement of values.

The key questions that this study seeks to answer are does the public have meaningful values, and if so, why are they are so unstable? What are the sources of instability in the values expressed by the public and what are the implications for American politics and public policy?

This book builds on research I performed for my Ph.D. program in Government and Politics at the University of Maryland. I had initially planned to use existing survey data and statistical methods to study values. My advisor suggested I first go out and talk to some real people to better understand how the public thinks about values. This turned out to be the most fascinating part of my research project. While I did ultimately develop statistical models of values using logistic regression analysis and structural equation modeling, the in-person interviews generated the most interesting insights and are what are reported here.

This book draws on extended, open-ended interviews I conducted with 31 people about their values. Over a period of six months in late 2005 and early 2006, I conducted in-person interviews around the Washington DC area and in

Rockingham County, a rural area in Virginia about two hours from Washington DC. While this fieldwork shows a detailed snapshot in time that is now more than a decade old, I believe it is still highly relevant to understanding public opinion today and the complex issues involved in measuring values in surveys.

Conducting these interviews was a truly an amazing experience. I travelled to neighborhoods in DC where I would not ordinarily go, and wondered whether it was safe for me to be there. I drove out into rural areas of Virginia where I often encountered distinctive cultural perspectives on values issues. I learned something from every person I met with. Most of all, I learned never to presuppose that I knew what someone would say. People were quite open with me, often relating very personal details about their lives. I walked away from this experience with a new appreciation of how complex public opinion is, and an understanding of how surveys used in social science just scratch the surface.

A simple question sparked my interest in the study of values. What is it that makes people believe the things they do? This question begets many more questions. At the individual level, how can people make sense of the political world when it is impossible for one person to have all of the knowledge that would be required to make fully informed decisions? How can individuals who share the same background, education and knowledge come to such disparate conclusions about politics and policy?

Many scholars have noted the general lack of political information held by the public as a problem for modern democracy. How can popular government function when the public knows so little about the key issues of the day? How can public beliefs and attitudes measured in surveys have meaning if they are subject to constant change, revision and flux?

These questions are important to me because I ultimately believe that public beliefs are substantive. Most individuals do have deeply felt beliefs that serve to make their political opinions meaningful, significant and reflective of underlying truths about social reality. The study of values would seem to provide answers to some of these questions. Core values serve as a foundation for individual beliefs. These values serve as overarching beliefs that help people make sense of the world. Even if values may simplify the decision making process for some individuals, they also engender a significant amount of complexity. Values conflict with each other. Which values are most relevant? How should you apply them? The context of a social situation may influence what values we hold. Within this framework, the nuances, inconsistencies, paradoxes and quirks of public opinion are significant. They are important because they demonstrate the tensions and lines of conflict that exist, not only within our own culture, but also within us.

There are five chapters in this book. Chapter 1 provides an introduction and review of some of the literature on how scholars have understood public opinion. This includes studies of ideology, values, belief sampling and non-attitudes. Researchers have struggled to characterize public opinion. Do values, ideology or something else shape public opinion? If values are so crucial, why is it that the same person asked the same values questions at different times give completely different responses? The next three chapters rely on in-depth interviews with subjects and qualitative analysis. Chapter 2 examines how the value of limited government is measured. Chapter 3 studies the value of moral traditionalism, while Chapter 4 is a close study of the value of equality. Each of these chapters examines the complexity and nuances of values. They reveal how each of these values is multifaceted. Many in the public are conflicted between values and within different dimensions of these values. The public is ambivalent in many cases. It is the attempt to reconcile incommensurable value elements, and not ignorance, which is the cause of this ambivalence. Public opinion vacillates, not because individuals do not care, but because they have deep-seated feelings that are both positive and negative about their own values.

Overall, this research shows that values serve as a foundation for public opinion, but that this foundation is intricate, complex and not easily reducible to simple causal relationships between different elements of the public's value system. In many cases, the public is ambivalent in their values. The social context, and the way specific issues are framed and linked to values, are an important determinant in shaping public beliefs.

Acknowledgements

There are a lot of people to thank for their help in making this book possible. First, I'd like to thank Jim Gimpel, my advisor at the University of Maryland, for helping me to focus this effort and providing key insights into managing and conducting the research for my dissertation. His knowledge, patience and enthusiasm for the subject were an invaluable resource. I would like to thank my committee members Fred Alford, Karen Kaufmann and Irwin Morris, who all provided input and comments that helped to improve the dissertation, parts of which served as the basis for this book. In addition, I thank my employer ICF for encouraging professional development and employee publications. Many thanks to the interviewees who volunteered and made this study possible. Last, but certainly not least, I thank Sarah O'Rourke for reading draft chapters and urging me forward. As always, while I thank others for their help, any errors or omissions are my own.

About the Author
Laurence O'Rourke is a public policy consultant at ICF, where he engages in multidisciplinary research on transportation, energy and environmental policy issues. He writes about a range of issues associated with public policy and governance. He is also the author of the book "Great Debates in American Political Science" as well as numerous journal articles, conference papers and reports on public policy issues. He obtained his Ph.D. in Political Science from the University of Maryland and an M.A. in Government from Johns Hopkins University.

Chapter 1: Values or Ideology?

This study examines the role of values in the belief systems of individuals. Historically, scholars have argued that the public organizes their opinion around a liberal-conservative ideological divide. When research uncovered the general lack of political knowledge and ideological thinking among the public, scholars began to search for other substantive sources of public beliefs. Many scholars have argued that values serve as the substantive anchor that makes public preferences meaningful and significant. Nonetheless, there has been significant debate over how substantive values are, how much information is required to use them, how values relate to each other in value systems and what the sources of instability are in values. This chapter sets the stage for examining values by reviewing some of the literature on ideological thinking and the role of information and values in public opinion. The search for a replacement for ideology has driven the interest of scholars in studying values. It thus makes sense to start this study of values with a review of the role of ideology in structuring public opinion.

Overview of the Literature

Every influential theorist of democracy begins with the idea that the public has meaningful beliefs and preferences about politics. Work in the field of political science has often struggled to reconcile the theoretical demand that citizens have meaningful preferences with the fact that much of the public pays no attention to politics and possesses little information about the major issues of the day. Public attitudes measured in surveys are often subject to substantial response instability, suggesting that they lack substance.

Political theorists have often conceived of politics as a clash of competing ideologies, with the public divided on liberal/conservative or other ideological dimensions. Early survey research on public opinion quickly deconstructed this view of the world. In their study of the 1956 election, Campbell, Converse, Miller and Stokes revealed a public that displayed almost no ideological reasoning. They analyzed respondent answers to open ended questions about their likes and dislikes of the major parties and candidates. They found that only 2.5 percent of their sample responded to politics in an ideological fashion that would rank issues according to a liberal and conservative scale.

In *The Changing American Voter*, Nie, Petrocik and Verba examined public opinion between 1964 and 1972 and found a marked increase in ideological constraint among the electorate. Voters became increasingly ideological and polarized in their political views during these years. The cause of this, they argued, was a political context that presented voters with distinct choices. Unlike the 1950s where the Eisenhower Administration sought to pursue a moderate agenda, the politics of the 1960s was more contentious. Starting with the election of 1964, where Goldwater offered conservatives a choice, not an echo, voters where confronted with new issues that polarized the electorate. Issues such as race, the war in Vietnam and Watergate divided the nation along ideological lines. They note, "The way in which people think about the political world is not merely the result of their social and psychological characteristics — the education they have or their cognitive capacities. The way people think about politics is also a reflection of the stimuli offered to them by the political world: the nature of issues, the salience of these issues, and the way in which issues are presented" (Nie, Petrocik and Verba 1999).

Later research noted that changes in question wording and enhanced efforts to identify voters with no opinion explained some of this increase in ideological consistency

(Sullivan, Pierson and Marcus 1978). Nonetheless, political context is critical to how voters view what politics is about, and shapes how they think about and relate issues to each other.

One way of conceiving of ideology is as a system of attitude constraint. Ideology limits the range of ideas and policy attitudes that a person is likely to hold. The more ideological a person is, the easier it is to predict their opinion on one issue based on their opinion in another area. Converse identified three types of attitude constraint, logical, psychological and social (Converse 1964). Logical constraint means that certain beliefs logically entail certain other beliefs. In general, logical constraint has typically been rather weak, with the specific elements of different ideologies combining in radically different ways over time. Social constraint occurs when learning and elite cue taking socialize individuals into a particular set of beliefs. Those who are most politically knowledgeable are familiar with how elites package policies together. As political knowledge increases, individuals become more consistent in the way they put together belief systems because they are more likely to know how elites have constructed their belief systems.

Political awareness also enhances ideological thinking because it changes the way one processes incoming information. John Zaller's belief sampling model of opinion formation provides a more fully developed explanation of why the politically aware also tend to be more ideological in their views about politics. John Zaller conceived of survey response occurring in a three-step model that involved receiving political communications, accepting them and then sampling from them when asked for an opinion. The more politically aware an individual, the more they were likely to be consumers of political information and receive political messages. At the same time, higher levels of information are also associated with greater resistance. "People tend to resist arguments that are inconsistent with their political predispositions, but they do so only to the extent that they possess contextual information necessary to perceive a relationship between the message and their predispositions" (Zaller 1992). Lastly, the more recently one has called a consideration to mind, the less time it takes to retrieve. When individuals respond to questions, they sample from the considerations that are available and produce an answer based on the number of considerations for and against a particular opinion.

Another important function of political awareness is that as awareness increases, public attitudes more closely approximate consensus or polarization among elites. Individuals respond to cues from elites, and they respond more favorably to cues from elites that hold views that are consistent with their existing predispositions. They can respond in an ideological fashion to elite views only to the extent that they know what elites believe, and are able to identify correctly whether these views are consistent with their own predispositions.

Overall, while the views of the most aware are more ideological and the level of ideological thinking in the electorates has varied over time, depending on political context, much of the public is uninformed about politics and often displays little ideological organization in their thinking about issues. Studies of public opinion have revealed it to be extremely unstable, suggesting that it lacks any substance. In his seminal study of belief systems, Converse found that on many issues, response instability was so high among the public in panel studies that he thought he could best explain them by completely random choice mechanisms. Converse speculated that a substantial fraction of the public did not have meaningful attitudes on most issues (Converse 1964).

Over time, scholars have offered several different critiques of Converse's non-attitude thesis. Achen argued that one must conceive of individuals as having a distribution of opinions rather than a single opinion (Achen 1975). Asking the same question repeatedly will yield a distribution of responses. The vaguer a question, the wider the distribution of responses that will occur. Thus, he argued that while response instability was a natural feature of public attitudes, measurement error in poorly designed surveys often made this problem worse.

V.O. Key took a somewhat different posture, arguing that the public had real preferences, but that these were often unfocused. On most issues, the public did not have well-crafted attitudes or specific demands for policies and programs. Rather, Key described public opinion as latent, serving to set vague boundaries within which policy makers could operate. The job of leadership was to seek to ascertain what these boundaries were, and then to define a program and convince the public of its merit. "Public opinion does not emerge like a cyclone and push obstacles before it. Rather, it develops under leadership" (Key 1960, 285).

In *The Nature and Origins of Mass Opinion*, Zaller developed a belief-sampling model of opinion formation that straddles between Converse's conception of non-attitudes and Achen's conception of attitude distributions. Zaller argued that respondents did not have "true attitudes" on particular issues. Rather, when asked for their opinion, individuals tended to sample from relevant considerations that were available at the top of their head, and provide an answer. Factors that change the mix of considerations that were relevant to answering the question cause response instability. Thus, question wording or question order might change the sample of considerations used to answer a question. In a similar fashion, news media coverage or political context might change which pieces of information were available or considered relevant to a particular issue.

Another critique of Converse's non-attitude thesis was suggested by Converse himself. While his article "The Nature of Belief Systems in Mass Publics" focused primarily on social constraint, he also identified psychological constraint as another source of the ordering of political ideas. He notes, "Often such constraint is quasi logically argued on the basis of an appeal to some superordinate value or posture toward man and society, involving premises about the nature of social justice, social change, "natural law", and the like. Thus a few crowning postures—like premises about the survival of the fittest in the spirit of social Darwinism—serve as a sort of glue to bind together many more specific attitudes and beliefs, and these postures are of prime centrality in the belief system as a whole" (Converse 1964, 211). Later scholars, who focused on the role of values in organizing political thought, further developed Converse's conception of psychological constraint.

In *The Nature of Human Values*, Milton Rokeach argued that individuals use values and value systems to form political attitudes. He believed that the values of freedom and equality were particularly important in shaping political beliefs. Scholars of public opinion have often relied on values as an alternative to ideological explanations for how public opinion is structured. Citizens who are too unsophisticated to possess ideologies nonetheless may have sufficient awareness to employ values to structure their attitudes and beliefs (Hurwitz and Peffley 1985). Values are more general and stable beliefs about the desirable goals of politics. These general beliefs serve as the basis for organizing one's thinking about politics. Value based reasoning can serve to reduce the amount of information needed to assess policies and form attitudes. A large literature has developed examining how and which values affect political attitudes. These include studies of the welfare state (McClosky and Zaller 1984; Kluegal and Smith 1986; Feldman 1988; Feldman and Zaller 1992; Feldman and Steenbergen 2001) as well as studies of racial policy (Alvarez and Brehm 1997; Kinder and Sanders 1996; Hurwitz and

Peffley 1992), post materialist values (Inglehart and Abramson 1994), affirmative action (Fletcher and Chalmers 1991), capital punishment (Norrander 2000), environmental policy (Pollock, Lilie and Vittes 1993) and many other areas.

In *The Nature and Origins of Mass Opinion*, Zaller offers two critiques of the values literature. First, many studies have failed to take account of the information required by citizens to use their values in generating attitudes and opinions. For instance, Zaller found that more aware members of the public with hawkish values were more likely to express support for aid to the contras than less aware members of the public with similar values. This was because it required a certain level of political awareness for citizens to connect their hawkish values to support for the contras. At a minimum, members of the public would need to know that the contras were fighting against a communist government in Nicaragua. When survey questions asked whether respondents favored using military power to stop the spread of communism in Central America, differences between hawks with low and high levels of information largely disappeared. Thus even value based reasoning requires the public to possess significant information.

A second critique that Zaller offers is that scholars have not specified any theoretical relationship between values and ideology. "The problem arises from the fact that, although numerous "value dimensions" between which there is no obvious logical connection, many people nonetheless respond to different value dimensions as if they were organized by a common left-right dimension" (Zaller 1992, 26). Different value dimensions relate to one's ideological identification in a loose way. These relationships tend to be stronger among those who are more aware. They are not strong enough to indicate that values can be organized according a single continuum, but they indicate that values are linked to each other in ways that are not intuitively, or logically obvious.

In *Hard Choices Easy Answers*, Alvarez and Brehm seek

to reconcile the divide between Zaller's belief sampling approach to opinion formation and the core values school of thought. They argue that both approaches are ultimately incomplete. The core values approach is insufficient because it "provides neither an explanation for opinions that are unstable, nor can it capture differences between masses and elites in the stability of opinion." At the same time, Zaller's approach "leads towards a model of citizens as exceptionally minimal in their core beliefs, citizens who make it up as they go along when asked to respond to opinion surveys" (Alvarez and Brehm 2002, 9). They argue that while public beliefs have a base in core values, respondents often have trouble determining which values do apply, or how they should apply them. Response instability occurs because of three different states: uncertainty, equivocation and ambivalence.

When a single value is predominantly relevant, but respondents have trouble determining its relationship to the attitude, their answers are often uncertain. In cases of uncertainty, response instability decreases as political awareness increases. More information allows respondents to more accurately link the issue to the value they hold.

Ambivalence occurs in cases where two core values conflict with each other. "Citizens face choices between desirable incommensurables---literally, that to accomplish one value requires annihilation of the other value—then that is a choice setting that is ripe for ambivalence" (Alvarez and Brehm 2002, 59). Ambivalence requires a choice between two distinct values that cannot be reconciled. Further, the choice must involve aspects of social life or politics about which the respondent cares. In cases of ambivalence, rising levels of political information and rising levels of value coincidence (the extent to which one's values are evenly balanced) lead to heightened levels of response instability, as the conflict between values is more starkly drawn by those who are most informed.

Equivocation is the third state that affects response

stability. Equivocation involves situations where two or more values mutually reinforce a particular attitude. In the case of equivocation, rising coincidence and rising levels of information, increase attitude stability.

Alvarez and Brehm suggest that choices that involve trade-offs between incommensurable values are rare. Abortion and euthanasia are two issues where the public appears to be ambivalent. In areas of racial policy, they find the public to be uncertain, while the public is equivocal in their attitudes towards the IRS. Nonetheless, political context also plays a role in defining what values are relevant to policy issues. "To the extent that elite cues are important in telling us what policy means (in terms of standing predispositions), the nature of elite debate becomes a critical force leading to ambivalence, uncertainty or equivocation" (Alvarez and Brehm 2002, 59).

Definition of a Value

The first step in studying the role of values in the formation of attitudes is to define more specifically, what the terms values and attitudes mean. A value "is an enduring belief that a specific mode of conduct or end-state existence is personally or socially preferable to an opposite or converse mode of conduct or end state existence" (Rokeach 1973, 5). Values differ from attitudes in that they are more durable and general. A value applies to multiple objects, while an attitude is a cognition about a specific object. A person might have many thousands of attitudes, but they would possess only a small number of values.

Attachment to equality is a value, while the beliefs that one should raise the minimum wage or introduce a more progressive system of taxation are policy attitudes. Values tend to be more stable than attitudes because they grow out of one's culture. Individuals derive their values from the institutions and social structure that make up a way of life. The generality of a value tends to limit the amount of information or reasoning required to obtain or maintain it. The stability of the institutions and culture that create values tend to make them more stable than attitudes over time.

In his seminal study of values, Rokeach analyzed 64 different values (Rokeach 1973). He distinguished between instrumental and terminal values. Instrumental values refer to modes of conduct that are useful in achieving desirable ends. These might include such values as ambition, courage, honesty, independence, obedience, helpfulness, responsibility and self-control. Terminal values refer to desirable end states, which would include things such as freedom, equality, family security, pleasure, self-respect or a world at peace.

Scholars further divided terminal values into personal "self-centered" values or social "society-centered" values. While salvation or peace of mind are personal values, national security and world peace are social values.

In our society, we typically teach and learn values in isolation from other values in an all or nothing fashion. At the same time, individuals hold multiple values. As individuals mature, they build value systems through which they develop a relative ranking of values. While an important feature of values is their durable nature, the relationship of values to attitudes is subject to change over time as individuals alter the relative weight that they give to each of their values, or as they acquire new values (Rokeach 1974).

Values play an important role in social and political life. Values serve as standards to tell us how to act and what to want. "A value is a standard that tells us what attitudes we should hold…it is a standard we use to justify behavior…it is a standard we employ morally to judge and compare ourselves with others. Finally, a value is a standard we employ to tell us what values, attitudes, and actions of others are worth or not worth trying to influence. If you claim to have a "value" and you do not want to influence anyone else

under the sun to have it too, the chances are it is not a value"
(Rokeach 1969).

Rokeach believed that two terminal values, equality
and freedom, could be used to define modern political
ideologies. Thus, he argued that conservatives valued
freedom more than equality, while socialists tended to value
equality and freedom equally. Communists valued equality
more than freedom, and fascistic ideologies tended to give a
low priority to both equality and freedom.

While the total number of values is small, the number
of permutations in the way that individuals rank these values
is very large. For instance, 18 terminal values have 18 factorial
different possible rankings, which creates 6,400 trillion distinct
value rankings. Similarities of culture reduce the number of
different value systems actually observed between and within
societies. Socialization by common institutions and
similarities of sex, age, class and race further reduce the
heterogeneity of value systems employed. Values stand as
intervening variables between cultural and institutional
experiences and specific attitudes. Values are thus the
dependent variables influenced by cultural forces, and the
independent variables that determine individual attitudes.

Holding a value does not predict only one possible
policy attitude. Values can conflict with each other, or the
different relative ranking of values in value systems can
predict a range of attitudes. Individuals may decide that
different values are relevant to holding a policy attitude.
One's level of political awareness may determine the ability to
reliably link values to attitudes. The way elites frame issues
may also change the values that the public perceives to be
relevant to a particular policy attitude.

A variety of values influence public opinion, these
include freedom, equality, ideas about limited government,
humanitarianism and moral traditionalism. I discuss each of
these below in more detail.

Individualism / Freedom

The value of freedom, or the right to make choices for oneself and to develop freely as an individual, is a fundamental American value. Thus, the Declaration of Independence declares life, liberty and the pursuit of happiness to be an unalienable right. Many consider freedom to be a fundamental element of what makes one human. Berlin notes, "But to manipulate men, to propel them towards goals which you — the social reformer---see, but they may not, is to deny their human essence, to treat them as objects without wills of their own, and therefore to degrade them" (Berlin 1969, 137). Mill asserted, "The only purpose for which power can be rightfully exercised over any member of a civilized community, against his will, is to prevent harm to others" (Mill 1865, 9).

Freedom and individualism are closely related concepts that political theorists have often used interchangeably. De Tocqueville identified individualism as a core American value. Scholars have credited him with inventing the word individualism. Individualism has several different meanings, and it is important to distinguish between different types of individualism. Economic individualism is the commitment to merit as the basis for the distribution of rewards in society and the belief that hard work is a value in itself and we should reward it. Academics have considered economic individualism to spring from the Protestant work ethic. Economic individualism has been a significant feature of American political culture and society since the nation's inception.

The belief in social and economic individualism underpins beliefs in limited government. One must be free from government coercion to pursue one's interests. Socioeconomic individualism is the belief that people should get ahead on their own through hard work. Another conception of individualism relates to personal freedom and autonomy to achieve self-actualization, what some have called expressive individualism (Bellah et al. 1996). While expressive individualism is an important part of American culture, individuals associate policy attitudes more closely with the value of economic individualism.

De Tocqueville believed that individualism held dangers for democratic society. He notes, "Individualism is a calm and considered feeling which disposes each citizen to isolate himself from the mass of his fellows and withdraw into his own circle of family and friends; with this little society formed to his taste, he gladly leaves greater society to look after itself." American democracy bred individualists who "owe no man anything and hardly expect anything from anybody. They form the habit of thinking of themselves in isolation and imagine that their whole destiny is in their hands…each man is forever thrown back on himself alone, and there is danger that he may be shut up in the solitude of his own heart" (De Tocqueville 1969, 508).

Equality

De Tocqueville believed that equality was the dominant American value. He asserted that Americans taste for equality was so great that they would prefer equality in slavery (De Tocqueville 1969, 506). The Declaration of Independence starts with the proposition that all men are created equal. Despite many areas of glaring inequality, American political culture has always placed a high value on equality.

Some observers of the U.S. have argued that American society has separate domains where different values are preeminent. In the domain of social and political institutions, rights are distributed universally, and the value of equality is dominant. In the economic system, institutions distribute material goods according to the principles of efficiency (Okun 1975).

Individuals hold the value of equality dear for a number of different reasons. Libertarians believe that equality before the law and the equal and universal distribution of rights serves as a check on the power of the state. Others argue for the equal distribution of rights as a protection of society against the encroachment of market values. We separate society into domains that distribute rights to all on terms of equality in order to protect values that we cannot achieve through free market transactions. A third argument for equality is humanism. Individuals have certain rights and we afford these equally to all in order to preserve human dignity. What rights an individual requires in order to safeguard their dignity is an area where social theorists differ. Some thinkers, such as Rawls, argue that extensive redistribution of primary resources, such as wealth, income and "the sources of self-respect" are necessary to promote the full and free participation of individuals in society.

Equality thus has several different meanings, including legal equality, equality of opportunity and equality of outcome. While equality of opportunity is often associated with a belief in economic individualism, the desire to enhance equality of outcome frequently conflicts with the desire of economic individualists to provide differential rewards.

The line between the domains of legal equality, equality of opportunity and equality of outcome is often blurred. Thus, equality before the law depends, to some extent, on access to the resources necessary to hire legal talent, or the time and resources to understand and the law. The unequal distribution of social and economic resources which society bequeaths on individuals through birth or a privileged upbringing, affect equality of opportunity. American political culture has tended to be more receptive to the values of legal equality and equality of opportunity.

Humanitarianism

Humanitarianism is a well-developed feature of American culture. De Tocqueville noted that Americans were individualists dedicated to the pursuit of self-interest, but they employed the concept of "self-interest rightly understood", which led them to sacrifice some of their wealth to help their fellow man. A variety of studies have documented the charitable and humanitarian activities that still characterize and distinguish American culture (Wuthnow 1991). Humanitarianism is comprised of several different components, including a positive evaluation of others, concern about their welfare, and feelings of personal responsibility for others welfare.

Humanitarianism differs from other values, such as egalitarianism, in that it involves elements of personal involvement and feelings of connectedness to others. Humanitarians feel a strong urge to get involved with solving other people's problems. A sense of personal connection and empathy with others serve as a foundation for humanitarian's feelings. This differs from egalitarian values. Egalitarians thus might have an abstract belief about how the resources of society should be distributed, but they would feel less responsibility to take action to achieve this outcome themselves. While the beliefs of egalitarians might be motivated by an underlying concern for human welfare, they would have less emotional and personal content than those of the humanitarian. (Feldman and Steenbergen 2001).

Limited Government

The ideal of limited government has been an enduring value throughout U.S. history. Henry David Thoreau opened "Civil Disobedience" with a quote that has often been attributed to Jefferson, "That government is best that governs least". From the inception of the nation, the ideal of limited government has been associated with both restricting the sphere of government control, and distributing power to state and local governments. Alexis de Tocqueville believed that the taste of Americans for decentralized and limited government served to promote freedom and civic engagement among citizens. On the growth of centralized administrative power, he notes, "But I think that administrative centralization only serves to enervate the people that submit to it, because it constantly tends to diminish their civic spirit. Administrative centralization succeeds, it is true, in assembling, at a given time and place, all the available resources of a nation, but it militates against the increase of those resources. It brings triumph on the day of battle, but in the long run it diminishes a nation's power" (De Tocqueville 1969, 88).

De Tocqueville feared that democracy carried within itself the danger of despotism. The people would more readily allow the power of democratic government to grow, and they would naturally look to government to solve their problems. The danger of the growth of government power in a democracy was not that it would be brutal or tyrannical, but rather, that it "hinders, restrains, enervates, stifles, and stultifies so much that in the end each nation is no more than a flock of timid and hardworking animals with the government as its shepherd" (Tocqueville 1969, 692).

Politicians have closely related the ideal of limited government to the ideals of self-respect, self-reliance, responsibility, individualism and freedom. Speaking in 1964, Eisenhower noted "in far too many ways we are moving toward federal domination over almost every phase of our economy…this may give to some an immediate sense of material well-being and personal security. But it is dangerous to our future…what is stolen by paternalistic government is the precious compound of initiative, independence, self-respect that distinguishes a man from an automaton, a person from a number, productive enterprise from a regimented people" (McClosky and Zaller 1984).

In the modern era, the Republican Party has more forcefully put forth the ideal of limited government. The modern Republican Party's anti-government ideology grew from shifts in party philosophy first propounded by Hoover and Coolidge (Gerring 1996). In 1922, Hoover noted, "Bureaucracy does not tolerate the spirit of independence; it spreads the spirit of submission into our daily life and penetrates the temper of our people not with the habit of powerful resistance to wrong, but with the habit of timid acceptance of irresistible might" (Gerring 1996. 141).

Throughout U.S. history, attacks on the power of government and appeal to the ideal of limited government have not been restricted to the province of any particular party. Most modern political candidates find it profitable to be against "Washington bureaucrats". Reagan declared that government was not the solution, but the problem. Clinton announced that the era of big government was over. The rhetoric of limited government has often been undercut by the actual growth of government. Politicians have nonetheless found it necessary to appeal to this enduring ideal that is embedded in American culture.

Moral Traditionalism

Beliefs about the sources of moral authority play an important role in the value systems of most people. Many political theorists have argued that religious beliefs not only shape one's political attitudes, but also provide the cultural environment that makes possible the achievement of other political values. De Tocqueville asserted that the religious beliefs and mores of the American people, what he called the "habits of the heart", were a pillar supporting American democracy. "While the law allows the American people to do everything, there are things which religion prevents them from imagining and forbids them to dare…Religion, which never intervenes directly in the government of American society, should therefore be considered as the first of their political institutions" (De Tocqueville 1969, 292).

The religious beliefs of Americans allowed for the self-regulation of personal behavior and made freedom possible. "Despotism may be able to do without faith, but freedom cannot…How could society escape destruction if, when political ties are relaxed, moral ties are not tightened? And what can be done with a people master of itself if it is not subject to God" (De Tocqueville 1969, 294).

There is a constellation of religious values, but political scientists have often examined religious values focusing on three different aspects of belief. These include religious belonging, religious believing and religious behaving. Religious belonging refers to the affiliation of one to a particular religion, or religious denomination. Scholars measure religious believing by doctrinal orthodoxy, which refers to "the combinations of beliefs traditionally regarded as central to the acceptance of faith". These include beliefs about such things as "the sources of religious authority — such as the authority of Scripture — and the appropriate relationship of individuals to the divine — such as the necessity of adult conversion experiences" (Layman 2001, 56). Religious behaving refers to private ritualistic religious activity, such as prayer, and social religious behavior, such as attending services.

While religious beliefs have shaped attitudes towards politics throughout U.S. history, their role has changed over time. The effects of denominational affiliation on political behavior have historically been more important. Thus, Catholics were more likely to be Democrats, and mainline Protestants to be Republicans. Since the late 1970s, our political culture has increasingly divided those who have orthodox religious views from those who have liberal or secular views. "Thus, the important political differences are not between Protestants, Catholics, and Jews, but between the members of those groups who have conservative, or traditional religious beliefs and their counterparts who have liberal, or modern, beliefs and moral outlooks" (Layman 2001, 54).

As new issues, such as abortion and school prayer emerged in the 1970s, many came to see politics as a battleground in a culture war, which pitted those with traditionalistic moral beliefs against those who espoused a more liberal, relativistic, and tolerant (or permissive) view of social behavior. Speaking before the Republican national convention, Patrick Buchanan noted, "There is a religious war going on in this country, a culture war as critical to the kind of nation we shall be as the cold war itself, for this is a war for the soul of America" (Layman 2001). Beliefs in moral traditionalism are typically associated with conservatism, but they can often conflict with other conservative values, such as limited government. The rising importance of cultural issues in the last 30 years has resulted in religious values exercising a larger role in the formation of political attitudes than at any time in recent history.

While each of the values discussed above are complex and not easily captured in survey questions, numerous studies have employed measures to operationalize these concepts (Feldman 1999). The specific data items available from the NES to measure these values are discussed in more detail in the following chapters.

Prevalence of Values in the Population

Values are more enduring and general than attitudes. One comes to have values through the process of socialization. Differences in one's life experiences, culture, contact with institutions, experience of gender based roles, and other factors, all influence the values that one holds.

American political cultural embodies a liberal consensus that emphasizes the importance of freedom and equality. A cultural consensus around values is usually reflected in the data by rising levels of attachment to particular values as political knowledge increases. Politically aware individuals receive more political information from their environment, and tend to more fully learn the values around which a particular culture is based (McClosky and Zaller 1984). At the same time, conflict and polarization of political elites tend to be reflected by increasing levels of polarization among those who are politically aware.

Table 1: Attachment to Values by Political Knowledge

Values Question	Knowledge of Politics				
	Very Low	Fairly Low	Average	High	Very High
The government should guarantee jobs	2.8	3.2	3.5	3.7	3.7
Government should decrease spending	3.7	3.5	3.4	3.1	3.0
A problem with this country is that we don't give everyone an equal chance	2.6	2.8	2.8	3.0	3.2
Better if we worried less about equality	2.6	2.9	3.0	3.1	3.2
Its ok if some have more of a chance	3.3	3.3	3.4	3.4	3.3
Society should do what is necessary to give everyone an equal chance	1.8	1.6	1.7	1.8	1.7
Society would have fewer problems if there was more equality	2.4	2.3	2.4	2.5	2.6
We have pushed equal rights too far	3.0	3.1	3.2	3.2	3.3

* Source: 2000 National Election Studies Data

The data displayed in Table 1 above show there are some differences in the way in which political values are distributed. The table shows the average ranking for responses to different values questions. Lower scores indicate stronger agreement with a particular value, while higher scores indicate disagreement. For a number of questions, there are systematic differences in the way respondents at different levels of political knowledge respond. For instance, as political knowledge increases, respondents are less likely to agree with the proposition that the government should guarantee jobs and more likely to reflect the individualistic belief that people should get ahead on their own. Similarly, as levels of political knowledge increase, respondents are more likely to believe that Congress should decrease Federal spending.

Some of the measures of the value of equality of opportunity are also different across different strata of political awareness. Thus, the data suggest that more politically aware individuals believe that there is less of a problem with the availability of equality of opportunity for all, but they are also more likely to disagree that we would be better off if we worried less about equality. More politically aware individuals are also more likely to disagree that equal rights has been pushed too far. On a number of the equality indicators, the data show that there are no differences between those who are more and less aware, suggesting that there may be less consensus around certain aspects of the value of equality.

When the distribution of values is broken out by party identification, the results are more mixed. The attachment to economic individualism measured by the guaranteed jobs question increases for both Democrats and Republicans as political awareness rises. Aware democrats tend to be more favorably disposed towards government spending, while more politically aware Republicans are more opposed to spending. The results are mixed for most of the equality indicators. Among Republicans, the relationship between political knowledge and attachment to different measures of equality is weak or non-existent in most cases. Attachment to the value of political equality increases for Democrats as political knowledge increases.

The Stability and Durability of Values among the American Public

The core values literature in political science assumes that values are more durable and stable than attitudes, and that values form a substantive basis in which public opinion is grounded. Attitudes themselves may be unstable, due to the inability of individuals to link their values to their attitudes, or because of value conflicts. Some scholars argue that values nonetheless provide voters more durable and general predispositions that influence their political thinking.

While there appears to be no systematic comparative study of the stability of values and attitudes in the published literature, a number of researchers have touched on this issue in passing. In his seminal article on the nature of belief systems in mass publics, Converse found that public opinion on the government ownership of utilities and housing was very unstable, even though this comprises a core value on the role of government in society. Test-retest correlations of attitudes on government ownership showed correlations of only .3 (Converse 1964). The most stable attitudes were partisan identification and attitudes about school desegregation. Attitudes about government guaranteed employment, often used to measure the value of economic individualism, showed test-retest correlations of about .4, more stable than most attitudes, although not strikingly so.

Rokeach showed that aggregate public ranking of values over time was relatively stable (Rokeach 1974). Test-retest correlations of the individual value rankings were subject to significant instability though. Public rankings of the value of salvation were substantially stable over time, displaying a test-retest correlation of .6. The stability of all other value rankings displayed correlations of less than .44, with over half having correlations of less than .35 (Inglehart 1985). Inglehart has argued that there is significant measurement error associated with values questions, and that multi-item measures of values perform better.

Later work by McCann found evidence that the same elite cues that attitudes were responsive to also influenced values (McCann 1997). For instance, in the 1992 election, individuals who voted for Clinton were likely to become more egalitarian in their values. Those who voted for Bush came to display values that were more traditionalistic after the election. McCann argued that party identification shaped the values of voters. Individuals tended to adjust their values to be more in accord with the value stances prominently showcased in the presidential campaign.

Political Knowledge and the Application of Values

A long line of research has generally been dismissive of the idea that individuals use ideology to derive their policy preferences. The literature on the use of core values in political science posits a solution to the lack of political knowledge and ideological thinking among the electorate. "Core principles are sufficiently abstract to enable most people to derive more specific policy preferences in one or two policy domains. By drawing upon general beliefs relevant to one or two domains, most citizens can reliably figure out policy positions on the basis of how consistent these are with their more abstract core principles" (Goren 2000). A few basic cultural beliefs "enabled people who possess only inches of fact to generate miles of preferences" (Wildavsky 1987).

There is some dispute between scholars on how political awareness affects the use of core values. Zaller has argued that most scholars do not fully appreciate how much information is required for individuals to connect their values to their policy attitudes (Zaller 1992). The idea that political sophistication allows citizens to more strongly link their policy attitudes with their values is the expertise interaction model of public opinion. A number of researchers have challenged the expertise interaction model, arguing that political sophistication does not affect the use of values, or that its effects are limited to particular domains (Goren 2004; Goren 2000; Sniderman, Brody and Tetlock 1991).

Other scholars have argued that information plays an important role. "Even though there are foundations for public opinion in beliefs and values, identifying which value is relevant may not be obvious for the respondent. As a result, there is also a great deal of malleability and fickleness in public opinion. The malleability or fickleness may come from a simple lack of information about the issues or about how their values should matter for the issues" (Alvarez and Brehm 2002). For instance, elites often supply cues about which values should be applied. On the issue of nuclear power, informed citizens were more likely to use the value of equality in forming opinions about nuclear energy, an elite supplied framework (Pollock, Lilie and Vittes 1993).

The way an issue is framed has important effects on how citizens employ their values. For instance, in the case of campaign finance, the values of expression and equality conflict with each other. Individuals tend to balance these values differently, depending on whether they discuss issues in terms of specific groups, or more generally (Grant and Rudolph 2003). Issue framing effects significantly drive public opinion toward government spending (Jacoby 2000). Public attitudes towards overall levels of spending are more negative than when surveys link spending to particular programs. Individuals who are more attentive to the issue frames developed by elites will thus tend to use values to assess issues in a different manner than less sophisticated voters.

Many scholars have argued that opposition to welfare in the U.S. is driven by the racialization of welfare, the tendency of the public to view welfare recipients as being primarily composed of minority groups that are undeserving of support

(Gilens 2000). With respect to welfare policy, while education tends to increase levels of tolerance and lower levels of racial resentment, enhanced levels of education also are "associated with greater hostility to welfare among those whose negative perceptions do manage to survive the process of educational socialization" (Federico, 2004). Higher levels of political sophistication thus may help one to link values to policy views, and in some cases, may be associated with helping one to link affective judgments, such as racism, to policy attitudes.

Some scholars have argued that political awareness affects the use of values in two countervailing directions. Improved information may make an individual's values and opinions more integrated. Increased levels of information may help to improve the vertical linkage between general beliefs and specific opinions. On the other hand, more information may increase the differentiation of beliefs and ideas that are considered relevant to a particular opinion. More information may enable an individual to balance many competing considerations, values and beliefs against each other. The linkage between so many values and ideas and a given opinion may reduce the linkage between any one value and the opinion. More information may make individual decision making more complex, and hence less easy to predict based on any individual value (Sniderman, Brody and Kuklinski 1984).

A number of studies have examined the factors that affect judgments about what is procedurally fair in the absence of information about whether procedures are really fair. In general, when individuals lack information about the specifics of a procedure, judgments about fairness are related to whether they identify with the group that is responsible for designing the procedure. In addition, under conditions of uncertainty, judgments of fairness are associated with whether one likes the outcome of the procedure (Sparks and Durkin 2007).

Relationship of Values to Ideology and Political Context

Research has examined whether there are really differences in the high-level reasons or values that liberals and conservatives employ. Blader found that the values deemed important by individuals varied based on the political context. When values were thought to support one's political ideology, individuals tend to assign more importance to these values than in other situations where they might not (Blader 2007).

Scholars have argued over whether a clean distinction can be made between values and political ideology. A number of scholars have conceptualized moral values as having causal effects on political ideas. For instance, Kohlberg has argued that the moral beliefs of individuals can be characterized as passing through six distinct stages. Each stage of moral development is more sophisticated, complex and advanced than the last. Over time, individuals generally advance to higher levels of moral development, although most do not progress through all six stages of development (Kohlberg 1963; Rest 1975). For instance stage three of moral reasoning is conformity to conventional social role expectations. Stage four reasoning is adherence to conventional community and social moral conventions, and the laws of society. Stage five moral reasoning considers morality in the broader context of what is best for the long range welfare of the entire community. Stage six reasoning is characterized by its inclusiveness of a broad range of moral formulations and its concern for tolerance, justice and individual rights. For Kohlberg, individuals who reached stage five or six of moral reasoning were capable of stepping outside the conventional moral context of their own society. They had the ability to consider universal moral considerations that were common across all societies. Using Kohlberg's framework, a number of scholars found that stage five and stage six reasoning, what they called post-conventional moral reasoning, was associated with rejection of conservative political beliefs (Fishkin, Keniston and MacKinnon 1973).

A number of studies have challenged the concept of stages of moral reasoning and their relationship to political ideas. For instance, scholars have argued that what values and moral beliefs individuals say they hold has little relationship to how they actually behave in instances where moral judgments need to be made. The moral judgments people say they would make are driven by the desire of individuals to present themselves in a socially desirable light. A range of contextual factors can influence how individuals respond to questions about moral values. For instance, undergraduates who were told that their responses would be read by a professor of philosophy tended to use higher stages of moral reasoning than students who were told that their answers would be read by a business professor (Gibbs 2005). Subjects were also able to increase or lower their moral reasoning scores when asked to role play the perspective of a liberal or a conservative, suggesting that variations in moral reasoning are a function of the content of political ideas, rather than abstract stages of moral development that were outside of political context (Emler, Renwick and Malone 1983). Further, individual assessments of the virtuous conduct of others were not associated with their stage of moral development (Emler, Tarry and James 2007). Overall, a number of scholars have questioned whether values, and moral values more specifically, are separate, distinct and prior to political beliefs.

Overview of the Book

This book focuses on the measurement of three values that have been considered by scholars to be the most critical values in American political culture. The next three chapters employ in-depth interviews to explore how individuals think about the values of limited government (Chapter 2), moral traditionalism (Chapter 3) and equality (Chapter 4). The research used the battery of questions employed to measure values in the American National Election Studies (NES). The NES survey, funded by the National Science Foundation, has asked a battery of questions related to values for decades, providing a comprehensive time series measurement of the values of the electorate in the United States. This research advances the study of public opinion by systematically evaluating the sources of instability in the measurement of values. The last chapter provides overall conclusions from the research.

The key questions that this study seeks to answer are does the public have meaningful values, and if so, why are they are so unstable? What are the sources of instability in the values expressed by the public and what are the implications for American politics?

Chapter 2: Measures of Limited Government

A substantial body of social science research has argued that values play an important role in structuring political decision making (Feldman 1988; McClosky and Zaller 1984; Feldman and Steenbergen 2001; Alvarez and Brehm 2002). By definition, values are enduring and overarching beliefs that affect numerous more specific attitudes. A set of values helps individuals structure and generate numerous other preferences (Rokeach 1973). Analysis of the stability of the values questions in the NES has found that some values are not markedly more stable than specific attitudes (Converse 1964). Individuals who are asked the same question at different times in a panel survey will often provide different answers to the values questions regarding equality, economic individualism, the role of government or moral beliefs. Even within the context of a single interview, scholars have noted the tendency of individuals to equivocate and be ambivalent about core values like equality and limited government (Hochschild 1981; Feldman and Zaller 1992). The disconnect between the theoretical stability of values and the real life instability of values in surveys is notable.

In theory, values are stable because they are linked to culture and are transmitted socially. Social institutions and values have a reciprocal relationship. Social relations reinforce values and values reinforce social relationships. Social institutions encourage a specific way of looking at the world, and this world view serves to support institutions (Thompson, Ellis and Wildavsky 1990).

How can the theoretical stability of values postulated by social scientists be squared with the actual instability and ambivalence of the public in surveys and interviews? Do the values questions merely measure specific attitudes, or do respondents think about larger concepts when they answer these questions? Do multiple individual interpretations of these questions explain response instability found in public surveys of values? Are value conflicts at the root of public ambivalence? This chapter employs in-depth interviews with respondents to see how individuals think about the questions used to measure the value of limited government.

Explaining Value Instability and Ambivalence Regarding Limited Government

One explanation for the response instability in the NES values questions is that the questions themselves may be poor tools to measure values. Political science research has offered a number of other possible explanations, and these are briefly described below.

Vague questions may cause response instability. Some political scientists (Achen 1975) have conceived of individuals holding a distribution of opinions. The vaguer the question asked, the wider the distribution of responses that can be expected. Many of the values questions are fairly vague, and thus it should be unsurprising that responses will vary over time. Others have argued that response instability may be due to ambivalence and conflicting values. People are internally conflicted and their vacillating responses to survey questions faithfully reflect this (Hochschild 1981; Alvarez and Brehm 2002; Lakoff 1997).

Zaller has suggested that response instability results from individuals who interpret questions based on what's on the top of their mind. Often recent events or the most accessible considerations will influence how respondents answer. Individuals may easily change their mind at a later date when other considerations rise to the top (Zaller 1992).

Values questions can become linked to specific issues or have partisan code words. In some cases, partisanship can dominate survey responses. For instance Goren hypothesized that party identification served to mold survey response to some values questions in the early 1990s (Goren 2005).

Values may be so embedded in the psyche that individuals are hardly aware of the controlling beliefs that shape their thinking. Since people are rarely asked to describe and justify their first principles, their responses may vary considerably as they struggle to properly express themselves. This may be particularly true when they are required to cram their beliefs into the confines of pre-conceived survey questions developed by social scientists (Hochschild 1981; Lane 1962). Individuals may not have the sophistication and political concepts to articulate their experience. Ideological blindness can make it difficult for respondents to express themselves when their experience of reality differs significantly from the ideals that society has transmitted to them (Hochschild 1981; Bellah et al. 1996; Alford 2005).

Since spontaneous individual survey responses may be tied to unconscious thought processes, asking individuals to explain their answer may lead to ambivalence as they search for a reason to explain their "automatic" response. When survey response is driven by unconscious automatic processes, experimental methods that can measure automatic behavior directly may be needed. Such methods have included measuring response time latencies or conducting hot cognition experiments (Burdein et al, 2006).

Political context can influence the extent to which individuals develop well defined and stable beliefs and values. For instance, the presence of immigrants in a community may serve to more sharply define individuals' beliefs and values regarding tolerance (Gimpel et al 2003). Those from more homogeneous social environments may have thought less about this issue and ambivalent responses may result.

On the other hand, homogenous social environments may serve to reinforce beliefs. Heterogeneous environments may expose individuals to a range of beliefs and value systems, making them less sure of their own beliefs. Individuals moving between different regions may find themselves challenged in new social environments and more open to changing their mind about even strongly embedded partisan identifications (Gimpel 1999). Scholars have found that those exposed to heterogeneous political discussion environments are more likely to develop ambivalent attitudes towards candidates (Huckfeldt et al. 2004). Heterogeneous social environments that represent different values may encourage ambivalence about values in some cases as well.

Those with dense social networks may have more well defined values. In rural communities in particular, extended family networks, strong community ties and religious social connections can serve to develop and reinforce stable values (Elder and Conger 2000). Lastly, some have hypothesized that people don't have values in any meaningful sense. Responses are so variable that they might as well be random. Public beliefs, even about core values, are vacuous and lack substance (Converse 1964).

Is Limited Government a Value?

This chapter focuses on the specific value of limited government. In the works of some social scientists, this value is given scant attention. For instance, Schwartz does not identify it as one of the exemplary value domains (Shwartz 1992). Goren speculates that it might be considered a policy preference, or at most a proxy for the value of freedom and self-direction (Goren 2005).

Certainly the founders of the country believed limited government was an important, perhaps the central value around which American institutions were built. Limited government represented the ideal of voluntary association, Federalism, natural rights, checks and balances and protection from the abuse of power. Limited government provided for the conditions of freedom and allowed for the pursuit of happiness. Limited government is a positive concept because the purpose of limited government is to secure freedom. The founders believed that government must be limited in power if individual liberty was to be safeguarded.   The Declaration of Independence states that "all men were endowed by their Creator with certain unalienable rights". For the founders, government was limited by natural God given rights and the protection of these rights was the primary function of government.

The authors of the constitution believed that limited government also meant limited by a written Constitution, which was adopted by the sovereign people as their basic law. This law could be changed through the amendment process. The constitution enumerated the powers of government, and reserved the rest for the people. Limited government stood in contrast to the arbitrary use of power and coercion applied by the crown and its institutions of government. Numerous scholars still consider this to be a core value in American culture (Feldman and Zaller 1992; Boaz 1997). The interviews in this chapter would tend to support the idea that individuals have deeply felt beliefs about limited government.

Some scholars have argued that public beliefs about limited government are important, but public opinion is divided around two distinct and separate dimensions of limited government, one that addresses itself to government intervention in the economy and a separate set of beliefs regarding individual freedom (Maddox and Lilie 1984). Certainly political theorists have often argued that economic and social freedoms are inherently linked together. For instance, De Tocqueville believed that Americans' quest for economic equality could create a centralized state that would crush individual rights and freedom (De Tocqueville 1969).

Many scholars have argued that socialism is not compatible with freedom and democracy in the long run (Friedman 2002). The public opinion literature has found, unsurprisingly, that the public at large is not comprised of philosophers with integrated political theories. Lane discovered that the public's beliefs about authority, fair play and other political ideas were morselized rather than conceptualized. Public beliefs about politics tended to be composed of a tapestry of small pieces of different political ideas. Instead of having a single abstract theory of limited government or equality, the public held many conflicting ideas. Rather than having a single overall conception of political philosophy, they possessed morsels of political theory.

Employing quantitative methods, Bennett and Bennett found that ideas about limited government were largely unrelated to the public's ideas about civil liberties and personal freedom. Opinions about limited government exist in "splendid isolation" from other specific beliefs about the operation of government (Bennett and Bennett 1990).

In a study of public responses to big government, scholars have found that individuals tend to consider four related sets of ideas about limited government (Fee 1981). First, some individuals conceptualize big government as welfare, big spending and socialism. A second group considers big government to refer to corporatism and the rule of wealthy special interests. A third group believes big government means Federal control at the expense of state control. Lastly, a portion of the public considers big government as referring to the bureaucracy.

Frames of Reference for Limited Government

Over time, scholars have also noted that the frame of reference for discussing limited government influences how the public expresses this value. For instance, in 1968, Free and Cantril argued that public opinion in America was schizophrenic on the issue of the size of government. On an ideological level, the public was opposed to the overall expansion of government, but they tended to express support for government when discussing specific programs (Free and Cantril 1968). Research in the early 1990's on welfare also argued that there was no ideological support for the welfare state in America. Even liberals tended to be ambivalent in their support for social welfare programs (Feldman and Zaller 1992). In later research, Cantril argued that significant portions of the public were ambivalent regarding the value of limited government (Cantril and Cantril 1999). This large ambivalent public served as a swing vote that could fall on either side of issues related to limited government.

Feldman has argued that the public has one view of limited government when an issue is framed in terms of individual behavior and another view with respect to society at large. The public tends to endorse personal responsibility, freedom and limited government when discussing personal behavior. When they consider society at large, the public endorses programs that reduce overall social inequalities (Feldman 2003). The public is conflicted between the desire to support personal responsibility and the attractiveness of reducing social and economic inequalities across the entire population.

Other scholars have argued that the government program frame of reference is more important in determining support for limited government. The public is against welfare, but they support other non-welfare programs like education, environmental regulation and science. When the public says they are for limited government, they really mean they are for limiting welfare (Jacoby 1994; Jacoby 2005)

Partisan framing may also affect the extent to which the public expresses the value of limited government. During the course of the Reagan Administration, Republicans became less ardent advocates for limited government. When their own party controlled the levers of power, Republican partisans were less wary of government power (Bennett and Bennett 1990).

Research Method: In-Depth Interviews on Values

In order to understand how individuals interpret questions, a sample of respondents was interviewed to discuss at length how and why they answered the values questions the way they did. This chapter describes my findings from a set of extended interviews. The interviews focused on respondent reactions to the limited government questions in the National Elections Study. I have conducted 31 interviews with a wide variety of people. Due to sound quality problems on several of the tapes, only 28 or 29 answers were transcribed for most of the questions.

Recruiting Interview Participants

Participants in the study were recruited from two sources. First, ads were posted on the Washington DC Craig's List, a free online classified directory. The ad offered respondents $20 to participate in a one hour interview regarding their general attitudes about government and society. The respondents were fairly diverse in terms of their age, geographical location in the DC area, and their background. Interviews were conducted with individuals living in Bethesda Maryland, Silver Spring Maryland, College Park Maryland, Washington DC, Alexandria Virginia and Arlington Virginia. The interviews were conducted in-person, and occurred in many different locations, including coffee shops, a public library, a school recreation center, apartments and individual houses. Respondents ranged in age between 20 and 60, with an average age of 41.

To obtain a more diverse set of respondents, individuals were also recruited with an ad in the Daily News Record in Harrisonburg Virginia. Harrisonburg is a small city of approximately 50,000 located at the center of Rockingham County Virginia. Rockingham County is a rural area in the heart of the Shenandoah Valley where 75 percent of the voters went for Bush in the 2004 election. Traveling on Interstate 66 and Interstate 81, one can cover the 130 miles from Washington DC to Rockingham County in about two hours. The area is picturesque, set against the mountains of Shenandoah National Park. Rockingham is one of the top counties for poultry farming in the U.S. The largest economic sectors in terms of employment include educational, health, and social services, retail and manufacturing. The median household income in the county in 2004 was $45,238, fairly close to the national average. Harrisonburg is home to the Eastern Mennonite University as well as James Madison University.

Interview Protocol

The National Elections Studies uses a number of questions to measure the values of individuals. The interviews I conducted involved asking these questions, and then following up with a series of questions that probed for additional detail. For instance, interviewees were asked why they had responded the way they did, and what the question, or specific terms in the question, meant to them. The responses were open ended and I recorded and transcribed these responses.

Many of the values questions are vague and it was unclear to me how individuals might interpret them. One goal of conducting these interviews was to obtain an understanding of what these questions mean to respondents, and what respondents were thinking of when they answered.

Interpreting the Results of In-Depth Interviews

In-depth interviews provide a wealth of information, and allow the researcher to get a more complete understanding of how respondents think about survey questions. This method of research is time intensive. Because of this, sample sizes are often relatively small. The small N available in these types of studies makes it difficult to extrapolate the findings to the population at large. Although my interviews were coded and some quantitative statistics are provided, the primary function of this research was not to directly generalize these results to the entire population.

Researchers that use in-depth interviews have identified a number of functions that this type of research serves. First, information from in-depth interviews is interesting in its own right, and the reader "can make judgments about its wider applicability on the basis of its resonance with his own experience" (Hochschild 1981). Thus in-depth interviews can suggest truths about public beliefs, but it can't prove them.

One can consider an in-depth interview to be a kind of case study. In-depth studies of particular cases can be used to develop questions for further research and puzzles for theory (Yin 1994).

In-depth interviews can provide information that is unavailable from surveys. "In opinion polling, the researcher infers the links between variables; in intensive interviewing, the researcher induces the respondent to create the links between variables as he or she sees them" (Hochschild 1981). The less structured format of an in-depth interview allows subjects to explain how ideas are related to each other.

Lastly, some have argued that in-depth interviews can generate findings that cannot be discovered through survey research. In-depth interviews provide a wealth of qualitative information that is unavailable from surveys. They can allow the researcher greater insight into the often complex and ambivalent beliefs of research subjects. They can help the researcher understand the psychological framework that individuals use when they respond to questions. They also bring out the complexity of belief that is often lost in more easily manageable survey instruments. By allowing respondents freedom to discuss their beliefs, they can bring forth ideas that are lost when responses must be fitted into pre-conceived closed questionnaire formats provided by social scientists. This type of qualitative information is highly useful for generating insights and research hypotheses that can be tested further with survey data.

One danger of an in-depth interview is that it provides greater opportunities for the researcher to guide interview responses, or to bias the findings. Everybody has a point of view, and it is often difficult to maintain an objective demeanor. Respondents will often provide answers that they think the interviewer wants to hear. Further, most people can see issues from a number of different perspectives. Follow-up questions can thus often elicit modified views or different answers if they are perceived to be pushing the respondent to change their mind. In order to somewhat mitigate these issues, subjects were told that the interview was not "looking for any particular response, but just what you think about the issues." Follow-up questions were straightforward, objective and not designed to fish for particular responses. The following sections describe my interview findings for each question.

Is the Government Getting Too Powerful?

The first question was: "Some people are afraid the government in Washington is getting too powerful for the good of the country and the individual person. Others feel that the government in Washington is not getting too strong. Do you have an opinion on this or not? If yes, what is your feeling, do you think the government is getting too powerful or do you think the government is not getting too strong?"

This question was included in the 2000 NES survey, but has been left out of subsequent versions of the NES survey. There was a substantial amount of confusion and uncertainty regarding this question. The question asked if individuals had an opinion and 7 percent, 2/29 said they did not. Another 17 percent (5/29) refused to answer, saying that they couldn't choose between the two options, since their response differed by policy area. Interviews were also coded for partisan references. A partisan reference was considered to be any mention of political parties, the administration or the President. Partisan references were fairly common, with 45 percent (13/29) using partisan language. This result suggests that respondents may have difficulty talking about the power of government in the abstract and often reach for a partisan frame of reference to answer this question.

Expressions of confusion about what the question meant were also common, with 14 percent (4/29) respondents identifying some component of the question as confusing. This is also interesting in that it may indicate that some response instability related to this question may result from the interpretation of the wording and meaning of the question. A number of different ways that respondents interpreted the question are discussed below.

What Part of Government is Too Powerful?

In general, the question was a difficult question for many respondents to answer, because while it obviously refers to the Federal government, people may like some of the things the Federal government is doing, but not others. One respondent noted, "I think in some areas the government is too powerful and in some areas the government is not strong enough, but I guess that is sort of, the typical conservative-liberal divide, where you want the government to be strong and powerful versus where you don't…" While some respondents said they would answer differently based on the domestic policy area, others said the difference between domestic and foreign policy domains was most important. One noted, "Well the Federal government doesn't do enough on domestic issues and it does too much on foreign aggressive issues."

Many respondents saw this question as dealing primarily with the question of civil liberties, and their responses focused on the expansion of government police power in the post - 9/11 world. Other respondents viewed this question as addressing civil rights, but they focused their response on the curtailment of religious expression in public institutions by the Supreme Court. The primary idea in all of these responses was that government power was not properly checked by law or some other higher standard.

Some respondents identified their response with a particular branch of government, and were explicitly partisan in the way they responded to the question. Their response that the government was too strong was actually a reference to the Republicans being too powerful. For instance, one respondent noted, "When I think of the government as too strong, I think of our government now as primarily a Republican government …..When I think of government, I immediately think of the White House, so if I think of government …maybe it's not the government that is stronger, but it is the White House". Some respondents also referred to the Federal government being too strong relative to state and local governments.

Too Powerful Is Defined by Representation, Checks and Balances

Others saw the government as being controlled by special interests and their response that the government was getting too powerful really referred to the power of these special interests in controlling policy. One noted, "you have to have a lot of money to really get satisfaction… it seems like a very selfish administration…it's not too me benefiting the everyday person like it should…"

Some respondents thought the question was really asking about how democratic the government was. One noted, "Here we're able to lobby, we're able to protest, and we're able to vote which is -- which a lot of people don't understand, you know, third world countries don't have that opportunity." Another answering that the government was not too powerful noted, "I think our checks and balances are still pretty much like in play and that's what the government is….it's not getting too powerful because we haven't lost our ability to swing government."

Thus responses suggested that there was a link between viewing the government as being representative and believing it is too powerful. Individuals who believed the government was responsive to the demands of the voters tended to believe that the government was not too powerful. Those who saw government as catering to the wealthy, wasting money, not interested in their well-being or as being dominated by special interests, tended to believe that the government was too powerful.

De Tocqueville believed that one danger of democracy was that citizens would have little compunction about ceding power to the state. When the state was "us", it was more difficult to object to expanding its scale and scope. Many respondents who believed the government was not too powerful did say that the government is "us".

Some of those saying government was too strong argued that government power was an inherently dangerous thing for citizens. One noted, "I think it was best summed up by Reagan, I believe, when he said that a government strong enough to do anything for you is strong enough to do anything to you". One interesting paradox is that some who believed the government was too powerful also argued in a later question that "there are more things government should be doing."

One possible explanation for this is that when individuals thought of the government as being too powerful, they were thinking of individual rights or different government programs than when they imagined additional things government should do. Another possibility is that individuals experience with different levels of government may also vary. For instance, one may think the Federal government was too powerful, but at the same time, find their local government responsive to their needs. Programs that have a local focus, like education, might be more popular than programs that have a national focus.

Thus there were substantial differences in how individuals interpreted what areas of government intervention this question addressed, what branch of government it referred to, and what political issues they were thinking of when they responded.

In summary, these results suggest several factors that may cause individuals to change their response to this question over time. There was some confusion over the wording and meaning of the question, specifically there was confusion on what government power referred to. The partisan frame of reference was commonly used for this question. As the party in power changes, individuals that are answering this question from a partisan frame of reference may change their response. Individuals were also significantly ambivalent because of their differing feelings about different parts of the government. Individuals appeared to answer the question using a number of different institutional frames of reference, discussing different parts of the government or different policy areas. Thus, if an individual initially responded to the question with regard to the executive branch, at a later date they might be thinking about the Supreme Court and respond differently. Lastly, the question was linked to individual beliefs about the responsiveness of government. Significant changes in external efficacy might also cause individuals to modify their belief about the power of government.

Less or More Government?

The second question asked respondents to choose between two statements. The first statement was "the less government, the better", while the second statement was "there are more things that government should be doing".

Many respondents who thought the government was becoming too powerful also thought that the government should be doing more things. Nobody thought that this was contradictory. One respondent thought the government should be doing more with the resources it had. She noted, "Because they are the ones who are spending the money that us taxpayers are paying year in and year out…and they are going, of course as you know, for war and things like that…and it's just an endless thing going on…it seems like we are losing more and they are just throwing it away…"

Approximately 66 percent (19/29) respondents said there are more things government should be doing. Respondents were asked what types of programs should be cut back or added. Once they had provided some specific examples, they were asked for a general reason why the government should do those things. Approximately 86 percent of respondents (25/29) provided general principals or reasons why government spending was either good or bad. For three of the respondents, their general reason was that they felt they were already paying for government services through taxes, but the money was being misspent on giveaways to special interests or wasted on foreign aid and military activity.

Overall respondents understood what the question meant. None of them expressed confusion about how to interpret the question. Approximately 21 percent (6/29) expressed ambivalence about how they should respond, indicating that they were torn or conflicted about their answer. Expressing considerations that could justify responding in either direction on the question was more common, with 41 percent of respondents (12/29) considering both sides of the issue while answering. Surprisingly, partisan references were not common. Only 14 percent (4/29) respondents mentioned the president, political parties or the administration while answering.

Paternalism

While most responses tended to focus on particular programs, some couched their response in more general terms. One made the case for a more paternalistic government approach by noting the following, "I think for the most part, individuals can't necessarily always make the most informed decisions, and have all the resources at their disposal to decide between 500 health care coverages, or 500 different schools, the government has too …has to attempt to provide a common denominator between everybody, because otherwise you have people without a clue, with no guidance from any sort of governmental authority".

One thought the government should take a more active role in helping people raise children. They noted, "We get guidance on our profession, on how to drive, but I just think about parenting for example. Like no one has stepped in there. No one has actually taught people how to eat correctly so they don't die of heart attacks. These are measures the government I feel should take. So I just don't think they're protecting the human interest..."

Compassion

A number of respondents expressed the general feeling that the government should care for its people. Just as one should be compassionate to others, so also should we want a government that also represents this ideal. One person noted, "I feel like we have a responsibility to help our own, you know, our fellow citizens and ...I just think it's really sad that there's so many people here, especially after Hurricane Katrina, it's obvious there are a lot of poor in this country who really need help and need help getting the tools and the resources to be successful...Some part of my purpose in life is to help other people and I kind of wish that the government felt more that way too."

Equality

The value of equality was also frequently linked to this question. Respondents believed that expanding government programs could help to reduce economic disparities in society that were unjust. Interestingly, only about 21 percent (6/29) respondents explicitly mentioned issues related to poverty in their response. Healthcare and education were more frequently referred to when discussing additional things the government should be doing.

Arguments for Limited Government

A number of respondents were ambivalent about a more active government in every area. One argued strenuously for a more active role in poverty programs, but then noted, "At the same time, why should the government be in the arts, why should the government be in religion, church situations, there has to be a separation somewhere, so should the government fund the arts, I'm not sure about that, it's kind of a fine line"

The most explicitly ideological response came from a self-proclaimed libertarian. He objected to the expansion of the activities of government outside of the target groups that were really needy. He noted, "The government has a role in so much and I think at some point there is individual responsibility that should take over in some cases and the government has taken over a lot of things that people traditionally have done themselves…There's an argument being made for all the social programs. Many of them are useful but I think in some cases they sort of overlapped beyond the group that they were originally intended for so people are getting benefits who probably don't need quite that level of benefit from the federal government. And people have become dependent, any problem we'll let the government solve it, let the government do it…."

Overall, respondents were less confused by this question. They referred to a wide range of specific issues, although health and education were typically mentioned. Partisan references were uncommon. Even when responses were partisan in nature, it was just as common for people to refer to bloated security bureaucracies or the war in Iraq as to discuss the growth of domestic social programs.

When discussing whether additional government programs were a good idea, many respondents referred to the efficiency of government, whether it was controlled by special interests and whether there was substantial wasteful spending by the bureaucracy. Their beliefs about the general efficiency and effectiveness of government were an important component of their general attitudes about whether additional government programs were needed. Since general beliefs about these issues are components of measures of external efficacy, changes in the strength of external efficacy should have an important impact on beliefs about the need for more government.

Can the Free Market Handle Complex Economic Problems?

The third question asked the respondent to choose between two statements. The first one was "We need a strong government to handle today's complex economic problems". The second statement was "the free market can handle these problems without government being involved." Several things are notable about response to this question. First, many respondents answered this question in the context of global economic considerations. Respondents also tended to define economic problems differently, and the question also brought out broader philosophical views about the relationship between the government and the market.

Most of the respondents answered that we need a strong government to handle today's complex economic problems, with 69 percent (19/29) responding this way. Almost all of the respondents, or 93 percent (27/29), were able provide a general principal why this should be. This may not be surprising since I used a very broad definition of general principle. For instance, discussions of market complexity, or the need for the government to help those less fortunate were considered to be general principals.

Respondents expressed ambivalence 17 percent (5/29) of the time. Expressions of ambivalence included people saying that it was a hard question to answer, or that they could come down on either side. Approximately 38 percent (11/29) discussed considerations in favor of both statements before answering. The question did not often evoke an explicit partisan frame of reference, with only 10 percent (3/29) respondents referring to political parties, the president or the administration. There was some confusion with regard to the wording of the question and what the terms in it meant. Approximately 14 percent (4/29) respondents were uncertain what the question was really asking. Issues of the day were very prominent in respondent's answers, with 90 percent (26/29) making reference to a current issue. This category was inflated by respondent's references to unemployment and economic growth, which were coded as issues of the day.

In a sense, this question asks respondents to choose between a status quo middle of the road option (strong government and the free market) and a more extreme option (only the free market). Interestingly, a number of respondents who still selected the free market option qualified their answer by saying that they still thought some regulation was necessary. These respondents tended to interpret this question as measuring their basic attitude about the free market, not a specific policy goal of eliminating all government regulation of business.

In general, respondents interpreted what economic problems were and what made them complex in different ways. Those who selected a strong government, tended to say that economic problems were complex because of social, environmental, safety, and other non-economic factors that were not addressed by market decision making. Alternatively, those that selected the free market tended to view complex economic problems as purely market related. Global economic markets moved too fast and were too complicated for effective government planning to master. A third category of response that was very common was reference to the lack of a level playing field in international trade. Many respondents argued that since foreign companies received aid from their governments, U.S. firms also needed such aid.

A number of respondents identified complex economic problems as economic need and the inequalities created by the free market system or government taxation.

One noted the following: "It sounds like money problems for the United States, saying that they are not getting better…maybe things should be distributed more evenly among people…its always one sided…you know they say the rich get richer…I mean I understand that…then more people could be upper middle class…they are just trying to keep pace with that …you know it's not benefiting everyone…the government wants more from the everyday person…you know they have given all they can ..It's just they want more and more…we are losing…"

Do you Trust the Government or the Market?

Respondents often had an innate trust for either the government or the market. While many respondents referred to the global market, and international issues, some thought the free market was better equipped to address global concerns while others found that globalization required more government involvement.

"I would go with two, I think the free market, they definitely have a pulse on what's happening, knowing more…I tend to think, it's not a paranoid feeling, but it is sort of a mistrust, people have their own personal agendas, more so I think, I feel sometimes in government, …in the open market, the free market, there is different thinking, there is a worldwide thinking, if that makes sense, ok"

Some respondents identified government programs as

forming the basis of the free market, while others saw the proper role of government as operating at the periphery of the market, dealing with problems that were not addressed, or created by the market. Preferring the free market, one person argued, "And maybe the government's role is to let the free market do what it does and then sort of go behind and deal with what doesn't get addressed by the free market or the free market cares not to do and then it would be a proper role for government to make sure that the people left behind who for example if there's an insurance issue, then the free market deals with people who have enough money to pay their premiums but if there are other people who don't have money to pay the premiums, then the government should step in and work with those and let the free market work for everybody who can afford."

Taking an opposite perspective, many respondents argued that the free market was built on top of government social programs. One person said, "if we have people out there struggling with their health, and struggling to better themselves education wise, and better themselves so that they have a roof over their heads how can our country be successful and compete with the rest of the world, I keep coming back to that, but that's how are we going to be economically successful."

Some respondents identified complexity as a key issue behind their response. They saw governments as ill-equipped to deal with complexity, or sometimes creating more complexity. The speed of decision making was important for one respondent, "…By the time the government gets around to reviewing it and making a decision regulating it, the issue has passed or it's no longer relevant, you make your own decision. Because of the time it takes for some things … the free market works much more efficiently in making quick decisions…"

For other respondents, the complexity of decisions was derived from their non-economic and social consequences.

One noted, "Yeah I think I would probably say that because while the free markets are bound with everything….economic problems and situations are inherently linked with social….all sorts of other situations in the world….so if you just leave it up to the free market, it will just kind of disregard anything that is not economic…"

The idea that the economy had a natural balance or self-correcting mechanisms that were desirable was referred to by a number of respondents. One noted, "I think it all balances itself out ultimately, and I think when the government starts meddling in it, it changes that kind of natural balance that will ultimately occur".

A number of respondents referred to the desirability of having the government make decisions and set the priorities for society. "I think there's a tremendous number of choices that have to be made at this point, and I think that's what you mean by complex economic situations. And so somebody needs to decide where the priorities are and to make decisions based on those priorities. And I may not agree with those priorities, but I think it is the responsibility of the federal government to make those choices."

For many respondents, this question was primarily about global trade. There appeared to be a wide variance in how individuals interpreted this question, defining complex economic problems in a different of ways. It was unclear to me whether answers differed because people saw the question differently, or if people chose to define the question differently based on their inherent predisposition toward one of the options. It seems likely that some response instability in this question results from changes in how individuals are interpreting what it means.

In general, one would also expect economic conditions to have an impact on how stable one's views on this question are. Respondents often referred to specific examples of plant closings and job losses in their communities. As such, it seems like the business cycle and regional variations in economic performance may have some impact on generating response instability.

Has the Government Become Involved in Things People Should Do for Themselves?

The fourth question that addressed beliefs about government asked respondents to choose between two statements. The first statement was "The main reason government has become bigger over the years is because it has gotten involved in things that people should do for themselves. The second statement was "The government has become bigger because the problems we face have become bigger".

Overall, 32 percent of respondents chose the first statement, government had become bigger because it had gotten involved in things people should do for themselves. One individual said neither, while the remainder selected the second option, "because the problems we face have become bigger". The question allows individuals to focus their answer on the statement that is most congruent with their beliefs. Thus for those who believed that government growth was a good thing, they tended to focus on the need for programs. Those who thought the growth of government was troubling typically focused on issues of bureaucratic inefficiency, personal responsibility, dependency and the negative results of government programs on individual behavior. Respondents were encouraged to discuss both sides of the issue, and 82 percent responded to problems becoming bigger, while 71 percent responded to the phrase things people should do for themselves.

The interview results were coded for references to partisan statements, issues of the day, general principles, statements of ambivalence, and statements with considerations on both sides of the question and whether respondents referred to welfare. Approximately 36 percent of the respondents referred to welfare when they answered, suggesting that while this question is linked to welfare, it is not just a proxy for individuals' attitudes toward welfare. Partisan statements were also not that common. Only 18 percent of respondents made directly partisan statements. Partisan statements were considered to include statements that referenced the political parties, the President, or the administration directly.

About 68 percent of respondents referred to general principles. General principles were defined to include references to the complexity of the modern world or freedom. References to "issues of the day" were slightly more common. About 71 percent of respondents referred to them. Issues of the day were defined to include issues recently in the news or issues that were currently on the public agenda. Thus for instance, issues of the day would include terrorism, social security reform or bird flu. If someone mentioned a historical issue, such as the formation of the FDA, this would not count.

Ambivalence was fairly common among respondents, with 46 percent of respondents making statements that conveyed the tentativeness of their answers. While some respondents were not directly ambivalent, they discussed both sides of the issue. A significant fraction, 61 percent, discussed considerations both for and against their answer. Again, this is not surprising as the follow-up questions probed the respondents for more information about their answer. Nonetheless, it confirms that many respondents could see both sides of the question.

The issues discussed were numerous, including both international and domestic policies. Most respondents referred to more than one issue, and many discussed multiple issues in different policy areas, suggesting that this question does tap a deeper value that can be applied to many different types of issues.

Interpreting the Question

Respondents interpreted this question in a variety of ways. Many individuals discussed the effectiveness of government programs, and the problems of having too much bureaucracy. Others discussed how modern society would be inconceivable without extensive regulation. Concerns about personal freedoms and the need for individuals to be self-reliant were important for some.

A number of the respondents had problems with how the question was phrased. They saw the growth of government as being the result of bureaucratic excesses or Washington insiders. Some argued that our problems might be bigger, but government had created some of these problems.

Bureaucracy

One respondent, who disagreed with both statements, argued that government had gotten bigger because of the nature of bureaucracy. They noted, "It's just incredibly, colossally, -- what's the word -- bureaucratic. You know, you've got your deputies, and your deputy agents, and your staff, and your this and your that, and it's totally needless. I think people -- they feel like a movie star. They want to have their entourage, you know. I think it's completely unnecessary. And when I read about the trips that these people are given and they take, it's just completely unethical. But I don't think they're really concerned about us".

Mistrust of the motives of politicians and bureaucrats colored the answers of a number of respondents. One said the following, "My own belief is that the reason government has gotten larger over the years is because government is a fabulously great racket for the tiny handful of insiders who profit from it....And that, of course, they have an incentive to grow government in size and power and dominance….And they can do that by promising benefits to the ordinary citizen. Vote for me and I will give you a bigger handout, you know, on these six programs that you happen to be signed up for….But I think the real explanation is the self-interested nature of those elites who benefit from government."

Government in Our Bedroom

Some respondents excluded moral legislation from their consideration in discussing this question since it did not "make government bigger". Other respondents thought this question referred directly to the regulation of moral behavior. These respondents measured the size of government by the range of personal behaviors it affected. For them, government involvement in things people should do for themselves was directly related to hot button issues such as gay marriage.

One noted, "Yeah, I am going to have to agree with that, because they are getting too much in their personal life…and that smacks of messing with peoples freedoms, and that's a little bit too much…the only people who need guidance are children, but when you are an adult you don't need somebody telling you what to do, as long as you are not doing something illegal, you don't need government in your bedroom or your house …that's too much…they are messing with freedom"

Self-Reliance

Limited government and self-reliance were linked together by a number of respondents. Taking personal responsibility and relying on one's own initiative were often contrasted with government programs that provided too many benefits to individuals without asking for anything in return. Often, those who had the least were the most adamant about the need to make it on your own. Relying on your own efforts was important, even when you might also require the help of other individuals or the government.

One interviewee noted, "Number one, my thing is that you get as much education as you can, because it is out there for you, publicly…go for it, study, stay on the straight and narrow path when it comes to education, and you will be able to make it…and you do for yourself that, and don't complain if you have to work a couple jobs, don't depend on the government, or government programs to do things, you know because when you are doing as much for yourself as you can then somebody can help you the rest of the way if you need the help, as long as they see you are trying and trying to do it, you are not trying to take from someone else, you do as much as you can, and if you need help, it will be there for you"

Another noted, "They help me with food stamps, they help -- I live in a rent subsidized apartment, and they have my son in the school lunch program. But I'm working. I could be sitting at home making a lot less money and I think it ought to be a requirement, like welfare to work programs so that we're not relying on them to take care of our bills. We're not relying on them to take care of all our kids. So go out and get a job."

One respondent argued strongly against the danger of dependency on entitlement programs. Government entitlement programs were dangerous because they were managed according to political expediency, and with little regard for the future. These programs reduced individual responsibility for planning for the future, but the collective political decision making that replaced them was a poor substitute. They said, "Well, one example would be the Social Security and Medicare and Medicaid systems in which people are told, oh, don't worry about saving for your old age and don't worry about making sure you have insurance and money to meet your medical costs because we in the government will take care of all of that for you…And to the extent that the suckers believe that…They are willing to turn over larger and larger amounts of their income and more and more of their decision making to this slick cadre of the elite who are promising to take care of them….And who can make good on that promise for a limited time because of the Ponzi nature of the financing. It has been possible for the promisors to take care of Social Security and Medicare and Medicaid recipients until the financial crunch comes. And, at that point, people who have trusted them to make good on the promise learn what every other sucker in a Ponzi scheme learns, that it only lasts until it crashes".

Ambivalence

Many respondents were torn between the need for the government to provide help, and the desire for individuals to rely on their own initiative. Even those committed to the need for a larger government didn't want the government "supporting everybody". They often accepted the existing order, but argued for incremental change. For some, the inability to target benefits towards the greatest need caused ambivalence.

One woman said, "And you see that on Katrina. And you know there are people that could do more. And I agree wholeheartedly. It is just hard to… to say who can and who can't. And you hate to make the ones that can't do better suffer for the ones that may be taking advantage of these programs and the free ride….Well, again, you see the people in New Orleans. I am just watching Katrina and everything and there is a lot of young, healthy people that were on welfare, didn't have jobs, no means. I don't understand that. But when you see the elderly and the sick and you understand that they needed that. I didn't understand why there were so many young people there that had nothing and why they depended on the government agencies for everything when maybe if you had to move someplace else and work, that is what you had to do. But I don't understand somebody that is able-bodied not to want to work."

Another form of ambivalence was shown by individuals who liked the goals of government programs, but disliked the excessive bureaucracy and the inefficiencies associated with public programs. One noted, "I think the problems have become more complex and -- but I think at the same time the government could be more efficient in the way they handled them...society has become more complex and therefore we need a bigger government, but that doesn't necessarily mean it has to be as big as it is. It could be smaller. They could help people towards helping themselves more as opposed to -- with less personnel and maybe in some cases not doing it for them but direct them to what they need better."

Federalism – Things the States Should Do for Themselves?

A number of respondents interpreted the question as implying Federalism. In their mind, things people should do for themselves referred to things states and localities should do without Federal assistance. One person said, "It means to me ...providing financial incentive to do things that you don't necessarily need financial incentives for.... There is a lot of the pork barrel spending...towns can get grants to build sidewalks...And towns and museums can get grants to expand their services....yeah, I guess just pork barrel projects....the government gets involved and things become more expensive than they need to be to serve the need....Building a bridge in Alaska to replace a ferry service that appears to be perfectly adequate."

Government Involvement Rorschach Test

Some respondents believed this question referred to government involvement with religion. Respondents interpreted the meaning of government involvement differently depending on their particular views. One respondent saw the government's involvement in stopping school prayer as an example of unnecessary government involvement. Another saw funding for faith based initiatives as unnecessary government involvement.

For many, government involvement in things people could do for themselves seemed to become a Rorschach test. Anything that one found undesirable about the government could be seen in this vessel. Thus respondents mentioned a range of issues, such as faith based programs, lawsuits to stop school prayer, gay marriage bans, pork barrel spending, unnecessary privacy regulations, financially unstable entitlement programs, the IRS and welfare.

On the other side of the coin, most people also believed that the problems we face have become bigger. Changes such as globalization, technological change, public health problems or homeland security, among others, were mentioned. In most cases, individuals could easily make the leap from the increased size and complexity of problems to the need for more government.

It appeared that the generality of the question easily allowed most individuals to develop responses to either statement based on a wide spectrum of specific issues. At the same time, most individuals were able to select a statement, allowing their natural disposition on the issue to emerge.

Overall, this question appeared to be a fairly good measure of people's attitude toward government programs. The question captures an important dimension of beliefs about government, specifically, what the balance between individual initiative and collective efforts need to be. It also captures an important component of individualism, whether one should be left alone to develop more freely as an individual, or whether perhaps one would benefit from greater guidance. This is an issue that cuts across the traditional liberal-conservative divide. This may be one reason why individuals displayed high levels of ambivalence when they answered.

Should the Government Guarantee Jobs and a Good Standard of Living?

The fifth question on beliefs about government was more focused on measuring economic individualism. Individuals were asked to respond to the following questions by placing themselves on a scale.

"Some people feel the government in Washington should see to it that every person has a job and a good standard of living. Suppose these people are at one end of a scale, at point 1. Others think the government should just let each person get ahead on their own. Suppose these people are at the other end, at point 7. And, of course, some other people have opinions somewhere in between, at points 2,3,4,5, or 6. Where would you place yourself on this scale?"

This question probes more directly attitudes towards government assistance to the individual. It was initially unclear to me how the specifics of this question would be interpreted. For instance, does the government "seeing to it that everyone has a good job" imply socialism and a centrally planned economy, or would respondents interpret that more generally to mean that the government should provide for the conditions that would create economic growth and provide opportunities for all? To what extent would individuals see this goal as being achievable by the government? How should a good standard of living be defined? On the other hand, does just letting each person get ahead on their own preclude government programs such as student loans? Where did individuals perceive the current U.S. status quo to lie on this continuum?

Interestingly, most respondents did not have trouble answering this question. Only one expressed confusion about what it meant. Many of the respondents understood the question to ask for comment about ideals that might not be achievable in the real world. For instance, a number expressed skepticism that it was actually possible for the government to guarantee a good standard of living for everyone. And on the other side of the coin, a number commented that it was never really possible to get ahead on your own. Everybody was the recipient of some help during the course of their life. Respondents did not seem to have any problem answering the question even though they might see their answer pointing toward an ideal direction that they would like society to move in. It was not necessary for either of the two options to actually be achievable.

Respondents answers tended to reflect the ideal nature of the question. All but one respondent addressed issues of principal in their answer. Only 17 percent of (5/28) responses used language that expressed ambivalence. (An expression of ambivalence might be that it was a hard question to answer because of conflicted strong feelings.) The relatively low levels of ambivalence found may be explained by the response format of the question, which allowed individuals to select 4 and be in the middle on their answer. Of the respondents, 17 percent (5/28) chose this option. Most of the respondents who selected this option valued both the ideals of self-reliance, and a government that provided for the economic requirements of its citizens. Overall, slightly more respondents favored the government guaranteeing jobs, with 43 percent (12/28) choosing this option. Only 39 percent (11/28) respondents selected letting each individual get ahead on their own.

Many respondents discussed both sides of the issue,

with 79 percent (23/28) referring to considerations both for and against their answer. Of the respondents, 45 percent (13/28) discussed what might be considered "issues of the day". Issues of the day would include concrete policy issues that were subjects of recent political debate and news coverage. These were defined rather broadly to include just about any policy issue. The fact that only 45 percent of respondents brought up issues of the day is notable, given the fact that many gave rather long answers to this question. Answers tended to be metaphorical, or focused on broad issues of human nature. Judgments about the nature of society, the economy and fairness were also common.

Only one of the respondents made statements that were partisan in nature when they answered the question. Partisan was defined as referring to the administration, political leaders or political parties. Only 14 percent (4/28) respondents referred to communism in their answer. A couple of other respondents made references to womb to tomb socialism or big brother. On the whole, most respondents didn't perceive this question to deal directly with the issue of creating a centrally planned economy.

Freedom

Respondents referred to freedom both when arguing for getting ahead on your own and for having the government guarantee jobs. One respondent arguing for the need of having government guaranteed jobs noted the following, "Because people become more free to make better choices, and be more creative and be more happy if those basic security blocks of life, the housing, the healthcare, their jobs are all taken care of, if those basic little security building blocks are taken care of… that is when things like the cure for cancer is discovered, and we go to Mars, Jupiter and Saturn, that's because people are spending so much time trying to make sure that they have housing and food, they are worrying about all those building blocks, they are never going to get up to that self-awareness, they can't become the best person they can be "

Another respondent argued for the desirability of self-reliance. Interestingly, he worked with homeless people, and volunteered in a homeless shelter. Nonetheless, he found the concept of government guarantees to promote a dependency that was ultimately damaging to the individual. For him, a good standard of living was premised on freedom of choice. He noted, "When I think of a good standard of living, I just immediately think that I have a lot of freedom to go and do what I want, to spend my money the way I want to, and I don't have the government telling me how to spend my money, that I have to buy a certain thing, that I have to do this, that I have to do that, ….I don't feel the government owes me everything, but I think everyone is entitled to make choices for a good way to live, now if you choose to live on the street, or you choose to live in a cardboard box, and you feel life is ok, I respect that, I respect that, that's your choice, but for the person that writes and complains, and doesn't have the economics that you or I have, I think there are ways that they can be challenged, and they have to challenge themselves, now I'm starting to philosophize, I just don't think the government owes me anything, it doesn't owe me a handout"

Some respondents saw government guaranteed jobs as a danger to freedom of choice. A system where the government controlled the economy and distributed resources was not consistent with the exercise of freedom.

"Getting along on your own abilities also means a lot of freedom to do what you want to do and in an environment that encourages that. You know, that's -- you know, we have a lot of options in this country. If we don't like the situation we can go out and change it yourself, a personal situation. You know, we're not assigned to jobs like, you know, in North Korea. We're not sent out to some weird piece of Siberia to mine gold or whatever, you know. …Well, I mean, that's your other side of the thing, you know. If we provide jobs to everybody the federal government is going to send them where there's a job, you know."

Ambivalence and Conflicts with Equality

A number of respondents expressed ambivalence. They saw economic inequalities as unjust and damaging to society. At the same time, they saw the necessity of inequality for rewarding good performance, and they disliked policies that were seen as too indulgent and not asking enough of the individual. A respondent said the following,

"I think that some people have a lot more than they need. You know, some people who are able to get ahead on their own. I mean, they have really expensive houses while other people have absolutely nothing. And I just think, you know -- on one hand, you know, I do believe if you have talent -- if you have a skill you should be, you know, rewarded more than if you don't, but I -- sometimes the disparity is just, you know, too much. And I think that it would help…I think the government should do a whole lot to make sure that people have a good standard of living, but that they don't have to give everything to everyone on a silver platter."

Some respondents were torn between the opportunity they perceived the market to provide and the inequalities and suffering that economic competition created. One said, "It kind of depends upon how I feel each morning almost, how grim the newspaper looks. There's so much opportunity and yet there's so much suffering, folks that are being left behind. I guess I would be maybe point three or something like that."

One respondent argued that it was desirable for each to get ahead on their own, because when most citizens were self-reliant, resources could be targeted to those that really need them. He noted, "The goal would be to empower as many people as possible to "get ahead on their own" whatever that means because then again it's more likely that that you can help those truly needy ones rather than sort of offering this pot of gold to everybody in that continuum. The result is since the resources are always limited you can only help either very thinly a lot of people or very deeply just a few people."

Many respondents viewed this question as a referendum on inequality. While some features of the ideal of self-reliance might appeal to them, the inherent social inequalities that burdened the disadvantaged self-reliant person made this option untenable. For them, the value of equality was more important than any type of market efficiency or personal freedom that getting ahead on your own might imply. One respondent noted the following.

"I really do feel that people should be -- should hold some level of accountability for themselves. I just think that there are some people who are born into positions or families, situations, economically privileged or whatever that put them at a different standard and I think it would be really naive of me to say that -- because I grew up in a middle class family that provided me with lots of opportunities to become well educated and I have as much chance of being a success as someone who is born into poverty."

Conflicts between Capitalism and Policies to Promote Equality

The belief in individualism and capitalism was fairly strong among many. Respondents often perceived economic individualism and capitalism to conflict with policies used to promote equality. A number of respondents noted that capitalism requires a system where there are no guarantees. It is only under conditions of competition for uncertain rewards that individuals put forth their best efforts. Guaranteeing everyone a job would erode the incentives that promote economic growth.

One respondent noted, "I think capitalism doesn't work if competition isn't there…if competition isn't there the people aren't constantly vying against each other to do the next best thing or to do the next best thing for their paycheck…So it's to the benefit, in the interest of everybody."

Another said, "Giving people stuff doesn't work because all it does is make people mediocre because once they have stuff they don't need to work for it. People need a drive, they need some reason to succeed and do better."

Measuring Extreme Viewpoints

The question allows respondents to place themselves on a scale to identify the level of their agreement with each of the two statements. One individual appeared to hold very intense libertarian views. He wanted to abolish the Federal Reserve, and he was vehemently opposed to social security and other government programs. Nonetheless, he placed himself as a 5 on the scale, arguing that he was not an anarchist. He believed the government had a role in providing for the common defense, and securing interstate commerce.

Another respondent chose to designate themselves as a seven on the scale. When they responded, their answer was a fairly moderate response, typical of that given by many who placed themselves in the middle. In this case, the respondent had just returned from Europe, and they contrasted their views with those held in Europe regarding the welfare state.

Interpretation of where your views lie on a scale requires two distinct pieces of information. First, you need to define what you believe, but also important, you need to compare yourself against what others believe. Geography, social context or exposure to political media thus may affect perceptions of what common political beliefs are, and how one measures their own intensity of belief.

Attachment to the Idea of Self Reliance and Work

Individuals perceived a conflict between self-reliance and government programs to guarantee jobs. For many, self-reliance and the virtues of work were seen as having positive moral and psychological benefits for the individual. A number of respondents argued that government guarantees were undesirable because they take away the pride of accomplishment one gets from working. For these respondents, material gains achieved through hard work were more satisfying than those that were guaranteed. One respondent discussed how earning a million dollars as an entrepreneur would be more inherently satisfying than winning the lottery. One noted, "if you go and work hard and do something yourself, the satisfaction of doing that is always a lot more fulfilling than if someone hands it to you." Another noted,

"Well, you know, if you are guaranteed a standard of living, what difference is that from welfare. You know? If you have done it and you have achieved things on your own and you have a pride there of what you have done, what you have accomplished, I just don't think the government owes you that, I don't get that."

Respondents obtained a non-material benefit from "making it on their own". Their enjoyment of the material benefits was related to how they were achieved.

Religious Language on Both Sides

Respondents answering the question employed religious language to both argue for getting ahead on your own and also for having the government guarantee jobs. One noted, "I think that's an area where government could do a lot better and should. I think that we are our brother's keeper and if we see somebody who has nothing and we have so much that it would be nice if every rich person can take care of those who are less privileged."

Another noted the following, "You do the best you can for yourself…it means to go out and get yourself more education. It means working while you are getting that education, I think that is what you have to do….I don't think big brother ought to have to provide your life for you. I think God made you to do the best you can on your own."

Religious language was not typically employed by respondents, and my general impression was that religious views were not closely linked to views about self-reliance. Most individuals did express the general belief that economic rewards should be allocated based on merit. The idea that "getting ahead on you own" was something to be valued outside of the economic rewards associated with it was also often present.

The fact that religious language could be deployed on either side of this debate is consistent with other research that shows religious beliefs don't always serve as a force for homogenizing disparate populations. "Religion acts more as a reinforcer of community values than as a transformer of them" (Gimpel et al. 2003). General beliefs on this question are likely to vary significantly between denominations, levels of religious observance and regional context. In some cases, religious beliefs and religious social networks may conflict with other elements of the social environment. In this context, they could serve as an important source of ambivalence.

Impossible Ideals

Many of the respondents selected between guaranteeing

jobs and getting ahead on your own, even though they perceived these options to be ideals. They argued that, in reality, these ideas were impossible. One noted, "Well, I don't think anybody really gets ahead on their own. I think somebody is always helping them. Somebody offers the opportunity …everybody gets a hand up by somebody….So, getting ahead on your own is really a misnomer. You know, it really doesn't exist. I mean it is like pulling yourself up by the bootstraps. I mean that is an impossibility."

Another argued, "Because I don't know where that's possible to get ahead on your own unless you're -- you've got magic tricks up your sleeve. A general, honest hardworking person is just going to work themselves right to the grave. They're never going to get ahead. Some might get really lucky. I don't know, that's how it feels to me. It just feels like life is just a big struggle and even though you work hard and pay your bills there's never enough left over to get ahead. The cost of living constantly increases but the wages don't."

Many respondents were also skeptical that the government could solve all economic problems by guaranteeing jobs to everybody. One said, "Well, that means communism basically or communism as it played itself out in the Soviet Union. Everybody will have a job, everybody will have the same standard of living, but it probably won't be that good and it will get worse because nobody will really want to succeed. So, you know, you just can't make everybody have a good job. That's crazy. Everybody can't make $50,000 a year doing stuff. It's not going to happen."

Thus the choices offered where ideal goals, or myths for those who disliked the choice. For many respondents this did not pose a problem. In the same breath that someone would say that guaranteeing everyone a good job was not possible, they would also say that it was a direction that society should move in. While a respondent would agree that pulling yourself up by you own bootstraps was an impossibility, they would also argue that this was something that should be aspired too.

These results were reminiscent of Hochschild's findings in *What's Fair*. In her in-depth interviews with subjects, she found that many individuals did not believe that it was possible to achieve a major redistribution of wealth through implementing socialist policies. She notes, "Most people do not seek downward redistribution because they cannot imagine it or do not believe in its possibility. Those who acquiesce do not endorse the dominant pattern of beliefs in American society…they perceive no other set of beliefs available to them" (Hochschild 1981, 278). For Hochschild, it was a failure of imagination that prevented socialism in the U.S.

The findings from my interviews are somewhat different though. Individuals tended to be fairly conservative when it came to their ideas about policy. When faced with rendering a judgment on "guaranteeing jobs and a good standard of living for all", they tended to asses it as an ideal that should be worked towards, usually through implementing fairly mundane incremental policy solutions like providing training or promoting job growth in the private sector. The ideal was worthy, but implementing socialist policies were not the first solution they reached for. Similarly, while most know that "pulling yourself up by your own bootstraps" is by definition impossible, they nonetheless have no problem aspiring to this as well. The ideal of self-reliance could help to improve the behavior and fortunes of individuals, even if it might never be attained. In this sense respondents were imaginative in their thinking about values, but pragmatic in the way they linked their ideals to what they saw as "the real world".

Freedom and Potential

In some cases, individuals were guided by their social imagination more than their economic reality. For some, getting ahead on your own represented an ideal of freedom. Even though they might not get ahead themselves, one was freer living in a society where this was still possible. One respondent noted, "Well, I mean, you should have the opportunity to get ahead. I mean, any -- everybody ultimately has the choice of doing whatever they want. I'm not really very competitive and I'm not in a career where I'm really going to ever make any money. Well, that's fine. I'm a teacher and I'm going to be a youth minister when I finish graduate school. I'm not ever going to make any money I 'm never going to be, you know, one of those people that have gotten ahead. It's just a matter of, you know, if I wanted to I could. ….And I've been successful in a number of different fields and it's worked out really good. If I'm interested in something I can usually go after it without too much trouble. That's what -- I guess the potential of getting ahead is the important thing. There's always people that don't want to get ahead and that's fine. There's nothing wrong with that either."

Self-Reliance and Character

When discussing why it was more important for individuals to get ahead on their own, respondents often referred to the character building function of self-reliance. "Getting ahead on your own" taught individuals the value of money. Struggling to get by taught individuals how to manage their lives. Overcoming obstacles gave them a sense of their own worth and confidence in their capability. Struggling to make it taught people to value what they did have. Respondents often discussed the value of getting ahead on your own in the context of teaching children to be adults. One noted, "I mean it is like a kid. If his allowance is a dollar a week and he doesn't have to do anything for it, then you know, so what if I blow a dollar….But if he has to take out the trash, walk the dog to get his allowance, then it means something."

Having the government guarantee jobs was like an indulgent parent that gave their kids everything they wanted. Ultimately, the parent kills them with kindness, and they never face the types of challenges that would allow them to grow up. One respondent noted the following, "Because if you don't show your own initiative -- it's like a child whose parents have done everything for them and the day they're out of college they have no idea what to do. They don't have to balance a checkbook, they don't know how to manage money, they don't know how to save for the future, they don't know anything because they get handed the money the entire time. They've never had to manage anything…You put these people in decent jobs and give them a house, what's to say they're going to keep their decent job and that house? They didn't work for it. There's not an initiative.…But it's okay to get a little help as long as you're pushing forward as much as you can."

Some respondents made the distinction between individuals relying on the government and relying on family or community social networks. In regions with strong social capital, such as rural areas, an individual might not need to rely on government guarantees for a social safety net. Strong family and community ties lower the risks of catastrophic social failures in rural communities.

In *Children of the Land*, Elder and Conger identified the specific values associated with rural farming. They note, "When parents and children talk about the virtues of living on a farm, they invariably mention basic values of this lifestyle — those of hard work or industry, self-reliance and a sense of responsibility, a commitment to family life, social trust and a value system that is not devoted to money and consumerism. People who depend on each other must learn to trust, as on farms and in small towns. The work ethic of farm life is valued for the confidence it provides young people who are thinking about themselves and the future, and what they can do with their lives."(p.52)

Interview results tended to confirm this characterization of rural life, and specifically the farming lifestyle. Respondents from rural areas did speak more eloquently about the virtues of self-reliance. While social trust and social capital are often conceived as a resource that increases the efficiency of government and allows for more effective governance, social capital may also serve to be a source of individualistic and self-reliant attitudes in some rural contexts.

Overall, this question appeared to tap important values. Rather than be confused by the vagueness of the question, most respondents were able to answer at length and to discuss their ideals. While the question focuses on the relative value of individualistic verses social economic behavior, the question also taps important dimensions of freedom and equality. From their responses, many individuals seem to believe that this question required them to assess the relative value of freedom and equality. Given the significant number of respondents who chose 4 or other responses in the middle, this was a choice many preferred not to make.

Discussion

Over time, scholars have argued different things with respect to the value of limited government. Some have suggested that limited government is not really an important value, but merely a policy preference, or only a proxy for other important values (Schwartz 1992; Goren 2005). Other scholars have argued that while limited government might be a value, there is so much measurement error (Achen 1975) or influence from contextual factors and top of the head responses (Zaller 1992), that current survey tools may not effectively illuminate a true belief about this value. A third possibility is that the public does have deep seated beliefs about limited government, but that ambivalence results from value conflicts.

Overall, the bottom line take away from my findings is that response instability toward the value of limited government is caused by value conflict within respondents. The public does have deeply ingrained beliefs about the value of limited government, and in many respects, there is a strong tendency among the public to endorse libertarian ideas that link a belief in limited government with personal responsibility, freedom and free market capitalism. At the same time, these same values are seen as inconsistent with a longing to achieve more social and economic equality in society. While the founders of the country believed that equality, limited government and religious belief in natural God given rights were consistent and self-supporting values, many in the public today understand these values to be in conflict.

These interview results reinforce the research of a number of scholars who have found the public to be deeply conflicted about their core values (Hochschild 1981; Tetlock 1986; Feldman 2003). Unlike some scholars who have argued that value ambivalence is fairly rare (Alvarez and Brehm 2002), these interviews highlight how a substantial fraction of the public is conflicted between the value of limited government and equality. This conflict underpins many specific policy issues in American politics.

Most respondents were able to elaborate in a heartfelt manner on their beliefs about limited government. While the public's beliefs about limited government were deeply rooted and conflicted, there were also a number of separate dimensions of belief. Perhaps the most dominant interpretation of limited government was its association with personal responsibility.   Personal responsibility was often contrasted with dependence on government welfare programs. Limited government meant checks and balances for some, while for others it meant federalism and a greater role for local government. Limiting government power was desirable for some because they perceived the government to represent the power of special interests. A fifth dimension of limited government meant promoting individual rights and social freedoms. Gay marriage was frequently mentioned, but freedom of religious expression was also often cited. A final dimension of limited government was a mistrust of bureaucracy and its effectiveness in achieving social goals. These basic dimensions of limited government are similar to those found by Fee (1981), but individual rights and social freedoms were more prominent in my interview findings. Individuals often argued that common moral beliefs conflicted with the value of limited government.

While social freedom was an important dimension of limited government, religious language was found in both arguments for and against limited government. In addition, while those arguing for greater social freedoms often discussed the need to limit the role of government in restricting gay marriage, social conservatives often also argued for the need to limit the role of government in restricting religious expression. Even respondents who were not supportive of the value of limited government often articulated support for a specific dimension of this value. While some saw limited government as an inherent part of social freedom, others saw government enabling social freedoms.

A number of scholars have argued that the value of limited government and economic freedom exists in splendid isolation from the public's conception of individual rights and social freedom (Bennett and Bennett 1990). The findings from these interviews are somewhat different. While these values were related in my interviews, specific individuals often differed in how they related these concepts. The direction of the relationship between economic and social freedoms often differed between different respondents.

The desire to limit government was related to how representative people perceived the government to be. Unsurprisingly, the idea that the government "is us" reduces the desire of people to limit government power. As suggested by a number of scholars, the value of limited government was closely associated with the value of freedom more generally (Goren 2005).

Individuals used a variety of different government program frames of reference when they answered the question. Respondents not only discussed different government programs, such as welfare, education and health care, but also differentiated between different levels and branches of government. Some have argued that public endorsement of limited government tends to reflect a dislike of welfare spending, but not other types of government programs (Jacoby 2005). These interview findings were somewhat different. Respondents identified a number of different areas in which they thought the government should be limited. While these certainly encompassed welfare, they also included the arts, restrictions on gay marriage, spending on the war in Iraq, foreign aid and pork barrel projects.

The primary source of ambivalence among respondents was caused by a desire to promote personal responsibility at the individual level. At a more general societal level, respondents also endorsed the role of government programs in alleviating inequality. These findings are similar to those of a range of scholars (Feldman 2003; Feldman and Zaller 1992) who have argued that the public is conflicted between their endorsement of individualism at the micro level and their equally strong desire to promote equality at the macro level.

The limited government questions tended to evoke higher levels of partisanship than some of the other values questions. The control of government by a specific party made it difficult for some respondents to separate out their abstract feelings about limiting government from their specific feelings about the party in control. This is consistent with the findings of some scholars that Republican control of government tends to heighten the value of limited government among Democrats and reduce the importance of this value for Republicans (Bennett and Bennett 1990).

Globalization has had an important impact on ideas about the free market. Many respondents who endorsed the need for a strong government to handle complex economic problems cited the role of foreign governments in manipulating the terms of trade. The increased pace of globalization has played an important role in reducing the public's support for free market policies. When the free market is perceived to be dominated by foreign big business, many no longer understand free market capitalism to be consistent with the value of equality.

Hochschild has argued that American endorsement of limited government and their rejection of socialism reflect a failure of social imagination. While it is certainly true that most respondents rejected socialism, my results were somewhat different than what Hochschild found. In my interviews, respondents tended to be fairly imaginative when they conceptualized their ideals, but they were pragmatic and incremental when they sought to link their ideals to policy solutions.

Conclusions

Overall, these results support the idea that limited government is an important American value. The public's conception of this value is multi-faceted. Ambivalence with regard to this value is caused, in part, by a deeply embedded conflict between a desire for personal freedom and responsibility, which is associated with limited government, and an equally strong desire to promote equality throughout society, which is often linked to government programs to mitigate inequalities. Individuals were most conflicted when they contrasted their views about society at large, with a different set of standards which they applied to the individual.

The many different dimensions of limited government make it difficult to generalize about how this value is linked to specific policy beliefs. Much of the public's belief instability with regard to this value is related to how they frame an issue when answering specific survey questions. These results have several implications for politicians. First, libertarians who wish to make the case for limited government should frame their arguments in terms of personal responsibility. Support for personal responsibility and economic individualism is based not primarily on materialism, but in ideas about what is best and most natural for the development of good character. Because limited government is a multi-faceted value, different parts of the public may be responsive to other facets of this value as well, such as arguments about federalism, the bureaucracy, the rule of special interests and individual rights and social freedoms.

Somewhat paradoxically, for politicians who seek to expand government programs, it is best to appeal to broad ideas about social equality. At the macro-level, strong support for social and economic equality is related not to narrow self-interest, but to idealistic beliefs about what is best for all of society. It is the conflict between the ideal of freedom and responsibility, and the ideal of social equality that makes American public attitudes so dynamic and unpredictable.

Chapter 3: Measuring Moral Traditionalism

Some social scientists have argued that American politics has become dominated by a culture war (Hunter 1991; Wuthnow 1989). On one side are those espousing traditional or orthodox conceptions of morality. Traditionalists see morality as being based on external and transcendent sources. They believe in non-negotiable moral truths. On the other side of the cultural divide are those who espouse progressive moral beliefs. Progressives believe moral standards are relative and change with the times. They expect the boundaries of human knowledge and specific circumstances to alter the understanding of what is, and is not, moral.

The moral divide extends to ideas about the family and traditional lifestyles. The orthodox tend to see traditional family relationships as being based on a natural order. Those espousing progressive moral beliefs argue that it is a sign of progress that social standards and relationships evolve over time. William Bennett once characterized the culture war by saying, "America is divided between people who believe there's moral decline and people who say, what do you mean by moral decline?" (Layman 2001).

Is it true that America is divided along a moral fault line? Can members of the public be easily sorted into orthodox and progressive camps? Through in-depth interviews with subjects, this chapter seeks to cast light on how respondents think about questions designed to measure moral orthodoxy and progressivism.

Public Opinion and the Culture War

Hunter's book *Culture Wars: The Struggle to Define America* is a seminal work in the literature. The book developed more fully many assertions that have become central to the debate over whether a culture war exists in the United States. Hunter had at least five key assertions about the nature of the culture war.

First, Hunter argued that the center of conflict in U.S. politics was no longer critically defined by differences between religious faiths. Religious persecution has a long history in the United States. Catholics, Mormons, Jews and others have experienced significant persecution in the past because of their faiths. Historically, denominational differences defined key voting blocks in partisan coalitions. Thus Catholics and Jews tended to vote Democratic. Mainline Protestants were often Republicans. Beginning in the 1960s, differences between orthodox and progressive interpretations of the different faith traditions have become more important. For instance, today it is common to find orthodox Jews, traditional Catholics and fundamentalist Christians voting Republican in opposition to abortion.

Second, Hunter also argued that the orthodox-progressive divide was a central organizing principle of elite attitudes on a range of other issues not typically considered to be moral issues. For instance, those with orthodox moral views tended to have different attitudes about spending on welfare, healthcare, the environment and foreign aid. A much higher percentage of the orthodox believed that the U.S. was a force for good in the world. Those with progressive moral beliefs were more likely to believe that the U.S. did not treat the third world fairly (Hunter 1991).

Hunter also found that the orthodox-progressive split among the public influenced how individuals defined key values such as equality, freedom and tolerance. Those with traditional moral views tended to understand freedom in social and economic terms. For them, freedom was the condition that society enjoys when it does not live under despotism. Freedom exists when society is allowed to govern itself. It is not the unfettered freedom of the individual to do anything they want, but rather the positive freedom for an individual to freely achieve a common conception of the good. For many with traditional moral views, economic freedom is linked with social freedom. A society without control over economic resources will not long stay free.

Hunter argues that progressives understand freedom in negative terms, as a lack of political and social restraints on behavior. For progressives, freedom is defined by individual rights. Freedom is "a condition where an individual is granted immunity from interference by others in his life, either by state or church or other individuals."(Hunter 1991) Under this conception of freedom, being oppressed is the absence of choice. This conception of freedom is intimately linked with tolerance of diversity.

According to Hunter, the orthodox also differ with progressives on their understanding of justice. For moral traditionalists, justice is considered to be righteous adherence to higher moral laws. Laws ultimately draw their authority from biblical principles. Laws are just when they punish what is wrong and reward what is right. For progressives, justice means the end of oppression in the social world. Progressives conceive of justice as being intimately related to alleviating economic inequalities.

For progressives, the meaning of tolerance is to encourage moral pluralism and the understanding of the relative nature of all beliefs. Progressive tolerance seeks to celebrate different ideas about morality, seeing each of these ideas as having equal claim to respect and acceptance. Because the idea of moral relativism is in stark contrast to the orthodox moral vision, the orthodox often argue that social institutions and education based on moral pluralism are intolerant of their moral views. For the orthodox, a tolerant society is one that provides space for the existence of absolute conceptions of morality.

There are also disagreements over the meaning of America. It is argued that orthodox and progressive views define the meaning of American history and America itself in different terms. Those espousing orthodox views are more likely to subscribe to the idea of American exceptionalism. This view of history sees America as holding a special place in the world. The orthodox tend to believe that laws and governmental institutions are based on an authority greater than themselves. Rights come from god, not from government. Individuals are "endowed by their creator with certain inalienable rights."

The progressive vision of America is based on pluralism and diversity. This history focuses on the founders struggle to maintain a secular state that separates religious beliefs from political institutions. Progressives stress that the constitution was not based on absolute principles, but rather the Supreme Court was established to interpret the constitution as a living document that will change with the times.

Moral divisions are also manifested in how one defines the family. Moral traditionalists tend to see the family as being representative of a natural or divinely ordained order. For progressives, the traditional family was oppressive. One activist noted, "Where the women's movement has stood for equality, the bourgeois family has historically repudiated equality…Where the women's movement has called for the recognition of individualism, the family has insisted upon subordination of individual interests to the group" (Hunter 1991). Progressives thus seek to move away from the definition of the family based on biological relationships and towards one based on a conception of companionship, which allows for the validity of different family types.

Lastly, a key observation made by Hunter was that polarization along moral lines was driven by activists, who tended to have more extreme views on moral issues than the public at large. The culture war was powered by media technologies, political activists and cultural institutions which worked to translate and magnify its ideas. In later works, Hunter asserted that the concept of a culture war should not be tested with mass public opinion data, but rather with the tools of cultural structural analysis (Dionne and Cromarte 2006).

Other scholars believe that focusing analyses of the culture war on individual opinions is necessary to capture the important effects that public opinion does have on shaping politics (Wolfe in Dionne and Cromarte 2006). In contrast to the idea of a nation divided on cultural issues, these scholars have argued that the idea of a cultural war is a myth. Through analyses of public opinion data, they have sought to refute the thesis of polarization. For instance, Paul DiMaggio reviewed data from the General Social Survey and the National Election Study and found that with the exception of abortion, the nation had not become more polarized (DiMaggio, Evans and Bryson 1996). Through in-depth interviews with 128 subjects, Smith found that most people had never heard of the culture war, and disliked the idea of it when it was described (Smith et al. 1997). In *One Nation After All*, Wolf interviewed 200 suburban individuals from eight communities and came to the conclusion that if there was a culture war, it took place inside Americans and not between them. Most Americans believed in both traditional values and personal freedom (Wolf 1998).

In later works, even Hunter argued that most of the public, about 65%, held middle-of-the-road beliefs about abortion (Hunter 1994). The percentage of Americans holding extreme views on abortion has not increased in recent years either (Fiorina, Abrams and Pope 2006). Through analysis of the Survey of American Political Culture, Hunter and Bowman also described how the public could be classified into different categories with respect to their commitment to public culture. These included a number of diverse moral interpretations including pragmatists, conventionalists and communitarians (Hunter and Bowman 1996).

A somewhat related line of research has sought to test the proposition that moral issues have served as a cross cutting issue that has realigned the coalitions that make up the parties. Layman has argued that rather than displacing existing racial and economic conflicts, moral issues have extended political conflict to a new dimension. Party activists have become polarized on more issues, rather than reorganizing themselves based on cross cutting moral issues (Layman and Carsey 2002).

For some, the idea of a culture war defining a key political divide in U.S. politics implies that public views on moral issues are well developed and deeply embedded in the public psyche. Some scholars have argued that the orthodox-progressive divide shapes political behavior in many other countries around the world as well (Koster and Waal 2007; Barnea and Schwartz 1998).

The idea of public opinion being divided around orthodox and progressive beliefs finds challenge in much of the general literature on mass attitudes, which has argued that public opinion is ephemeral. For instance, Converse believed that much of the public did not have meaningful opinions on most issues (Converse 1964). Survey responses were merely doorstep opinions offered in an off-the-cuff fashion to satisfy the needs of researchers. They reflected little actual underlying belief or deeply felt opinion. In fairness, Converse did note that moral attitudes tended to be more stable than other attitudes. Nonetheless, they were still subject to significant instabilities over time.

Scholars have also understood public opinion as a reflection of a random sampling of the most salient considerations that happen to be accessible during the interview process (Zaller 1991). According to this conception, the ever shifting and inconsistent responses of the public to survey questions are a reflection of underlying beliefs, but this is highly sensitive to the timing and context of the survey.

Another possibility is suggested by scholars studying value conflicts. These scholars have argued that the public is deeply conflicted about their core values and how they should be applied to the political world. For instance, traditional moral beliefs may conflict with egalitarianism or humanitarianism (Keele and Wolak 2006). Social conservatism and moral traditionalism may conflict with freedom and individual rights (Barnea and Schwartz 1998).

Scholars have disagreed on the prevalence of ambivalence among the public. Some have argued that value ambivalence is fairly rare. Only in cases where one is faced with a choice that requires a direct trade-off between two deeply held and irreconcilable values does true ambivalence come into play (Alvarez and Brehm 2002). Scholars have typically argued that ambivalence is uncomfortable, and subjects try to resolve their cognitive dissonance (Festinger 1957).

More recently, some social scientists have revised this belief, arguing that individuals can comfortably live with many conflicting and inconsistent values and beliefs (Tetlock 1986). They are rarely confronted with situations where value conflicts come into focus. It may only be in cases where dissonant beliefs become simultaneously accessible where individuals will experience uncomfortable cognitive dissonance (Newby-Clark, McGregor and Zanna 2005). Scholars have also found that individuals are capable of holding both positive and negative beliefs about the same attitude object (Martinez, Craig and Kane 2002). Whether an individual says they feel ambivalent is often somewhat unrelated to objective measures of ambivalence collected through multiple survey questions (Priester and Petty 1996).

In stark contrast to the idea of a public polarized around moral issues is the possibility that individuals themselves are often deeply conflicted about their basic core moral values. They rarely systematize their beliefs into ideologies or consistent value systems. A significant body of research has been devoted to defining and measuring the ambivalence of the public. In-depth interviews are an important research tool to measure ambivalence. Survey tools may allow a researcher to speculate on the existence of ambivalence, but they cannot empirically demonstrate that a respondent is conflicted. In-depth interviews provide a format that allows the respondent to express conflicting beliefs and ambivalence toward core values.

Data and Methods

The American National Election Studies asks four questions that are commonly used to measure what political scientists have described as "moral traditionalism". In general, these questions measure attitudes towards traditional social arrangements and tolerance of different moral views and outlooks. The results of my in-depth interviews with respondents for each of these questions are described below. Twenty eight subjects were interviewed on tape to discuss their response to these questions. Individuals were initially asked the question, and then prompted with follow up questions to elaborate on why they answered the way that they did.

The research method used in this chapter is a qualitative analysis and presentation of the interviewer responses. The selection and characteristics of the respondents are discussed in more detail in Chapter 2. Qualitative research is obviously subject to more interpretation by the researcher. In addition, in-depth interviews may provide a greater opportunity for the researcher to influence the subject. Researchers may also have the tendency to focus their analyses on the most interesting and distinctive respondents. All of these factors introduce potential bias into the findings. In order to address these potential weaknesses, an interview guide was developed prior to the research to provide a consistent format to collect the information. The purpose of the guide was to ask questions in a sequence that did not solicit specific responses, but provided a neutral format that allowed individuals the maximum range to provide unsolicited feedback.

Selected interviewee responses to each of the four questions used to measure moral traditionalism are shown below. While some respondents could easily be categorized into a progressive or orthodox category, many gave nuanced and qualified responses that showed they were conflicted about their answers. In the same breath, respondents could argue for and against traditional moral beliefs.

Would Society Be Better Off with More Emphasis on Traditional Family Ties?

Individuals were asked to respond to the following statement: "This country would have many fewer problems if there were more emphasis on traditional family ties." Half of the respondents (14/28) either disagreed or disagreed strongly that society would have many fewer problems if there were more emphasis on traditional family ties. Only 43 percent (12/28) either agreed or agreed strongly. Two respondents neither agreed nor disagreed.

There were numerous interpretations of this question, and respondents varied considerably in what they thought traditional family ties meant. While some stated emphatically that traditional family ties were the most important thing in the world, others saw traditional family ties as representing an outmoded, authoritarian and archaic standard for organizing society. Many respondents were conflicted about family ties because they viewed traditional family ties as being representative of conformity and as restrictive of individual freedom. They also thought traditional family ties were unrepresentative of the diversity of society and repressive of other non-traditional relationships. Even when voicing these concerns, they also simultaneously voiced arguments in favor of the traditional family.

Interviewees expressed relatively little subjective ambivalence with regard to this question. Only 7 percent (2/28) respondents made a direct expression of ambivalence. On the other hand, approximately 32 percent (9/28) respondents discussed considerations both for and against traditional family ties. Only 4 percent (1/28) respondents made a direct partisan statement by referring to the President, the administration or political parties. This may under represent the actual level of partisan framing of this question, as a number of other respondents made statements that indicated a political interpretation of the question. Because they didn't refer to specific party labels, these were not coded as partisan.

There was some confusion on what the question meant, with 14 percent (4/28) respondents expressing uncertainty about what traditional family ties were. Reference to "issues of the day", were relatively uncommon, with 18 percent (5/28) respondents referring to common political or policy issues that one might read about in the daily newspaper. About 25 percent of respondents (7/28) referred to gay couples when they discussed what a traditional family tie was, and was not. Approximately 18 percent (5/28) referred to women staying at home with the children when they discussed traditional family ties. Another 25 percent (7/28) referred to religion.

Traditional Family Ties don't Exist Anymore

A common response of those who disagreed with the importance of traditional family ties was that it was unreasonable to expect to go back to some golden age in the past. They did not believe it was feasible to restore traditional family ties, and thus they rejected the premise of the question. When asked what traditional family ties were, one respondent noted,

"It means, you have to have a mom, you have to have a dad, you have to have grandparents, brothers and sisters, you have to have uncles and aunts, you have to belong to a church or synagogue, or a mosque, you have to have a lot of things…but our society doesn't have the luxury to provide that to everybody…so I think people need to think outside the box, to realize that because there are these huge market failures, if I can call it that, because there are these social breakdowns, if I can pull that in from the previous question, traditional cookie cutter, 1950s, traditional family unit just isn't there and things have to be looked at differently and thought about differently in the context of today's society, not in the context of something that happened 50 years ago.."

For a number of respondents, traditional family ties implied women staying home and raising the kids. Traditional family ties represented an archaic and old fashioned view of the world for some. It was neither desirable, nor possible, to return to this stable and constrained world. One respondent said, "Well, because I think traditional family ties could be interpreted to mean mom and dad married for forty years, you know, mom staying home and raising kids and dad going out and working and that is just not going to happen anymore."

Some respondents believed that emphasis on traditional family ties really referred to restricting gay marriage and gay adoption. Since they saw nothing wrong with these practices, they disagreed with the statement. One noted, "That's just another way of saying …something about marriage being limited to one man and one woman, some kind of concept like that. That's another rephrasing of that I guess, right? You know -- I don't see that as being the cure all."

Rebelling Against Family Dysfunction

As one might expect, the quality of respondent's

personal experiences with their own families affected their opinion of the importance of traditional families. Those respondents that had not had good experiences with their families often rebelled against them. One respondent said, "I was adopted, and was raised in a very dysfunctional family. My mother was a drunk. My father was very codependent. You can tell I have had a lot of therapy. Ahh, very codependent…both parents are now diseased, I'm gay, I had to go to church every Sunday because my father was Catholic, I was adopted from the Catholic orphanage and he signed a paper saying he would raise a kid Catholic…so for 18 years, traditional family values, I'm at church every Sunday and at 18 I rebelled, no more church, so we all lost… we all lose in those types of situations, I don't think families are the old tradition anymore…"

Traditional Family Ties Politicized

It was common for respondents to refer to "family values" when they responded to the question, even though the question refers to "family ties". This insertion of the more politicized wording suggested to me that these individuals were interpreting this question as having a more general political meaning. One respondent made this connection explicit when he disagreed with the statement because it had political overtones. He noted, "Well, I would say that I disagree with that, partially because of what "traditional family ties" has come to mean. If you had asked me that before the great emphasis on it politically, I might have agreed with it more, but now I would say I disagree with it… in the past it would have meant to -- staying within the nuclear family of whatever kind, our generation teaching other generations, and all of this I think would have been good. Now it means being more sort of the selfish, political jargon of those particular parts, and I don't agree with it. But it's become more of a religious and political football."

Focus on Traditional Families Shouldn't Crowd Out Other Options

An emphasis on traditional family ties was often interpreted as excluding or restricting non-traditional families. Even those who agreed that traditional families might be better, argued that the choice was not between traditional and non-traditional family ties, but between non-traditional and no family ties. One individual said the following,

"Well, you're talking about traditional families. You know, we need to open our minds about what a family is. You know, gays want to adopt AIDS babies, but a lot of people don't like gay adoptions but then there's nobody to adopt these people, okay. You know, many gay men will adopt African American children and if they didn't what -- you know, nobody is going to adopt.

You know, they say that the best family is a nuclear family, heterosexual with kids, and that that's where -- that's the best situation for a homeless child to be in or, you know, the best situation for a child to be in. That may be true, okay, but if the option for a child who is up for adoption is a nuclear family or no family, a gay family, a lesbian family, a non-traditional family would be far better, you know. So that's where I'm coming from."

Conformity

Traditional family ties were interpreted by some to imply conformity. One respondent, who neither agreed nor disagreed, thought the question was open to interpretations that he did not like. Traditional family ties were associated with a whole value complex that was conformist and which he did not necessarily agree with.

"Because I am afraid that traditional family ties would be interpreted to mean conformity. That we should all have short haircuts and shiny shoes and neatly pressed pants. I mean well who cares?...I think that the whole concept of the traditional family ties that are based on traditional moral values is aesthetic preferences disguised as genuine moral values. And mixed in with a small handful of what I would consider important moral values …like pay your bills, for example… Mixed in with that would be a huge amount of, oh, let's not have any more rock-n-roll music or rap music or whatever the current musical outrage is. I mean let's not have long hair. You know, just silliness that I think is of no consequence."

Traditional family values were seen as supporting arbitrary social hierarchy and authority. Traditional family values created a "Leave it to Beaver" world where "everybody is nice and polite and friendly all the time and no one questions anything." Under traditional family values, "everyone knows their place".

One respondent noted, "Because I think -- I guess I take that statement to mean … if more people lived in a nuclear families with the mom and the dad and all that and that people respected their elders more, that that society would maintain its hierarchical ways and that things would be better. And I don't agree…"

For some respondents, emphasis on traditional family ties suggested past oppressions and domestic violence. To imagine that a golden age of domestic tranquility had ever existed was to ignore a history filled with a whole array of other problems. The world where traditional family ties were dominant was also filled with social unrest, racism and sexism. One person noted, "We wouldn't have fewer problems, we'd have different problems. It's not -- I mean, people always like to look to the 50's as the golden age and -- you know, sort of "Leave it to Beaver". That never happened.

I don't know where we're getting -- you know, it's all right for husbands to beat the crap out of their wives all the time. You don't see that on "Leave it to Beaver", but it happened. Blacks and whites couldn't use the same drinking fountain, but that was the wonderful 50's. ...It's not that -- there would be different problems. Traditional family values provided a lot of problems as well. You need to have some sort of a balance in between, some sort of a flexibility because once you start setting anything in stone you're just going to get in trouble."

Freedom

For many, traditional family ties conflicted with freedom. Under traditional family ties, one was bound by custom, family obligations and arbitrary social conventions. Traditional family ties prevented individuals from creating social relationships and family structures that could secure their happiness. Speaking about traditional family ties, one respondent argued, "Well, it limits personal freedoms ...if that's the only thing that a family is under a traditional concept...it limits my personal freedoms, okay. It limits other people's personal freedoms. It's an outmoded concept which doesn't exist except in the minority in the United States.

Let's look at reality, okay. There are more divorced people than married people, okay. You know, the traditional family doesn't exist in reality or it does for the minority. And again it may be an objective, you know, we would like to have more married people, but reality shows us that it's -- that we're not, okay. You know, the non-traditional family is basically what exists in the United States, okay....Maybe 45 percent or 40 percent of the nation is in the traditional family, and that's good. I don't have any problem with that. But give me the personal freedom to set up a family situation that suits me and that provides my children with the same kind of education, personal growth, development, ...I mean, I came from a traditional family except we had eight kids, but that family is dysfunctional, okay. I don't see them because I prefer the family I set up here, even though I'm divorced, okay. It works for me and it works for a lot of other people. So that's why, you know, I would strongly disagree with that."

In another form of ambivalence about family values, some respondents thought more emphasis on traditional family ties was ok, but only if traditional family ties referred to positive family relationships. One woman noted, "I agree strongly if the family is intelligent and caring and loving towards their kids, but people who were in families where the parents are on drugs or indifferent to them or neglectful, then it's not true. But family ties should be increased -- families who are good to their kids don't need to increase their family ties because they already, you know, have strong ones."

While many respondents expressed frustration with traditional family ties, for others, they were the most important thing in the world. Traditional family ties embodied the values of selflessness and sacrifice. Being part of a network of family ties made an individual stronger and gave meaning to their life. One respondent noted the following about traditional family ties, "I think that they're the most important thing in life, in my life. I don't think there's anything more important. I think that when you have something else to work for than yourself that life is a lot more meaningful. I think that knowing that they're there gives me the confidence to keep going on even when terrible things happen. And it's just -- it feels good to be a part of something bigger than myself. You know, that -- to have other people who depend on me and who have an interest in me doing well and I feel the same about them. It's a great thing."

Reciprocity and Duty

Traditional family ties were described in terms of a set of reciprocal duties that were required of parents and children. Parents provided for their children, and it was the duty of children to respect their authority. When parents became older, it was the duty of children to take care of aging parents. One respondent described it this way, "your parents…raise you in an emotionally and physically stable and healthy life, I think you should obey your parents because they're older than you and I think they're wiser than you. And you should spend time with your parents, -- because say what parents would not do everything they could to ensure that their children are well rounded, successful human beings? And I think if they did that, if they raised you in that way, then you should reciprocate that and when they're older you should take care of them when they're getting older and more physically and mentally incapacitated. And when they know that -- or when you know that they will not have long for this world you should go and spend time with them because before you know it, they'll be gone, and then that will be the end…"

Some of those that thought there should be more emphasis on traditional family ties saw these bonds as creating a leveling effect that provided support for those that needed help. Rather than creating inequality, traditional family ties represented an ethic of sacrifice that worked to raise the fortunes of everybody.

"I think America obviously is an individual society. I'm going to go again with my background roots. People from third world countries are more family oriented and group oriented. They are not out there in the dog eat dog world. It's not survival of the fittest. You're very tied to your family. You're not trying to be out there trying to, beat other people or, you know, let other people drown, or be richer than other people and have them at the bottom end of society. Just kind of level things out and work with each other, improve everyone's life as opposed to just your own."

Some respondents struggled with what values should be passed on to a child. They thought parental guidance was important, but they also valued the idea that each individual must ultimately choose what type of person they will be. Ultimately, family ties were important in shaping what type of person they would be. They argued that traditional family ties prevented problems such as, "Dropping out of school, dropping out of high school. I guess living their lives through a series of low paying jobs. I guess going from boyfriend to boyfriend, girlfriend to girlfriend, changing partners all the time. Just kind of making do and not really getting anywhere….But, see, that's my value and it may not be theirs. That may not be their goal in life, you know, to make it in the corporate world. So -- but parental guidance, yeah, I think is absolutely important, absolutely, and I think that that's where a lot of parents fail. They provide the home and the food and not much else. It's really up to the kids to figure out, you know, how to navigate in adulthood."

Family Values Are Good, but Keep the Government Out of It

One respondent was ambivalent because they thought that emphasis on traditional family ties implied social or government policies. She thought that government action in this field was likely to be ineffective, or worse, cause greater problems. She noted, "I am for family values. But I don't think our society as whole should be dictating to people that you should have mother, father and children. And like in China where you can only have one child...I don't think that is the way to do it. But, for instance, like if there is a woman that gets to her thirties and she is not married and she wants to adopt and she can support the child, fine. Good and well...You know, that is not the norm. But I don't think as a society we should do anything to discourage the family or make it harder for families. But I don't think you can pass a law and say everybody go to church on Sunday."

Respondents interpreted this question in a variety of ways. While some thought the question related to gay rights or women staying at home with the children, others did not mention these subjects when they answered. It may be the case that some instability in response to this question is related to deeply held views about these subjects, and how the question is being interpreted. A number of respondents argued for both the importance of traditional and non-traditional family ties.

Most respondents were not explicit in expressing partisanship when they discussed their answer. While they lacked an explicit partisan reaction, respondents did often seem to understand that the question could have a political meaning. A number of respondents experienced a conflict between the objective and partisan interpretation of this question.

Respondents often discussed religion even though this question does not ask about it in any way. Traditional family ties were associated with general moral values for a significant fraction of respondents. Many of those who agreed with this statement were conflicted over how prescriptive the content of this morality should be. For many, personal freedom directly conflicted with traditional family ties.

Many of the respondents framed this question as a debate over what should be considered a family. Similar to the assertions of Hunter and other proponents of the culture war, what was at stake in this question was the very meaning of a family.

Are New Lifestyles Leading to the Breakdown of Society?

One of the questions used to measure moral attitudes on the NES asks respondents to agree or disagree with the following statement, "The new lifestyles are contributing to the breakdown of our society." Of those responding, 29 percent (8/28) either agreed strongly or agreed somewhat and 11 percent (3/28) neither agreed nor disagreed. The remaining 61 percent (17/28) disagreed, or disagreed strongly with the statement. Approximately 14 percent (4/28) expressed ambivalence about the question, saying that they were torn about how to answer, while 43 percent (12/28) discussed considerations for both agreeing and disagreeing with the question. There was some confusion about what the question was actually referring to, and 32 percent (9/28) of the respondents expressed uncertainty over what the various terms of the question meant. Partisanship was not frequently referenced and only 7 percent (2/28) of the respondents made references to political parties, the president or the administration in their response.

New Lifestyles: Code Word for Gay Rights?

Respondents were asked what new lifestyles they thought of. They did not interpret this question in any one way. Approximately 17 percent referred only to gay issues, 43 percent mentioned gay issues as well as other considerations and 40 percent did not mention gay issues when discussing what a new lifestyle was. It was fairly common for respondents to refer to family related issues when they responded to this question. Approximately 39 percent (11/28) of the respondents referred to heterosexual family issues, such as divorce and cohabitation before marriage. Approximately 14 percent (4/28) thought new lifestyles referred to women with children working. A number of respondents referred to new lifestyles as being driven by materialism, with 18 percent (5/28) of the respondents referencing this issue. It was fairly common for respondents to mention the bible or Christian values when answering this question.

Some respondents were angered by the question, seeing in it immediately an indictment of their lifestyle. One respondent who thought the question referred to divorce noted, "I just want to roll my eyes and vomit." Another noted, "When I hear that statement that sounds to me like it's a guy from the 700 Club talking about the immoral homosexuals and the homosexual lifestyle, and I think that's ridiculous."

While some interpreted this question as directly related to one's attitude toward gay people, other respondents saw in the question a broader array of issues. For these others, this question really addressed itself to whether social changes were undermining moral values. The question seemed to elicit respondent's general attitudes towards human nature. Some saw human nature as basically good. It was natural to expect progress in the future, and they saw new lifestyles as a natural process of social growth. For others, the freedom to select any lifestyle often meant that individuals made choices that were myopic, and did not consider their own, or societies long term well being

Another theme that came up during interviews related to respondents underlying posture towards life. Could the choices one made about how to live one's life be judged by a higher standard? Does an individual have an inherent purpose to their life, or could they freely select any lifestyle, as long as it didn't harm others? Were all these choices equally valid?

Some respondents questioned whether any lifestyle was new. One respondent noted, "I don't think humans have figured out in all this time new ways of expressing their humanity. I think these are things that probably get more coverage and I think we just -- we live in a society where there's lots of free time so people have time to think about these things. They're definitely not new. I mean, there's probably been a constant level of evil in the world or moral decay. I mean, I think in every age there's someone saying that things -- that things looked better before but it never -- it never was."

While some argued that the very notion of a breakdown of society was political fear mongering, others spoke in sincere terms of the evil that people could be capable of. One respondent noted the following, "Well, in our area, there is a lot of drug problems with methamphetamines and -- oh, gee, it is just awful. You see families tore up. And every week …and things that you wouldn't -- wouldn't think you would ever hear these people do for drugs."

Moral Dimensions of the Lifestyles Question

For many, new lifestyles referred to moral decadence. Respondents mentioned a wide range of issues both large and small, including drugs, abortion, sex on TV, premarital sex, obesity, consumerism, vanity, greed, spending beyond your means, materialism, instant gratification, infidelity, viewing pornography, cuss words on TV and people wearing scanty clothing. A range of family issues, both positive and negative, were also mentioned, including divorce, family fragmentation, children in day care, interracial couples, adopting children from other cultures, couples cohabiting outside marriage and single parents.

General considerations that respondents thought characterized some new lifestyles included political apathy, lack of concern for others, lack of concern for future generations, not making sure that children have the best lives possible and "everybody just doing what they want". Respondents also mentioned specific things that they thought were indicative of new lifestyles, such as fast food, Paris Hilton snorting cocaine, spending all your parents' money on prom dresses and the TV show "My Sweet Sixteen" on TV.

The question ties new lifestyles to the breakdown of society, and perhaps because of this, a majority of the considerations mentioned were negative. Other positive considerations mentioned included technology, online shopping, having everything at the tip of your fingers, freedom to move and to change one's life.

Some respondents who focused on morality saw new lifestyles as being in contravention of traditional morality. One respondent noted that people flaunted their "lifestyle in the face of the Judeo-Christian tradition. So -- and I think it's just horrible". Another said, "I go by the Bible that people -- people just aren't the way they used to be. They don't care anymore. You know, everything is just out there. Every little thing. It is just out there."

A number of respondents noted that a breakdown in moral values was a result of materialism and the mass media. One noted, "I think there's always been, I don't know, like decadent behavior, especially among the upper class all over the world. But I just think that with mass media and marketing of a certain image, people have strived to be -- I mean, I look around Starbucks here and I see people talking on their cell phones, drinking Starbucks latte, with the lap top, reading a trendy newspaper. It just seems like that that is an image that has been sold by our culture and people have bought it because it looks cool... why do people wear a Polo shirt with a Polo label on it... it's just vanity that says, yeah, I spent $65 for this shirt. ...what in our society is making people have that kind of mind set? ..The vanity of consumerism...."

Another conflated materialism and government spending with the loss of personal responsibility. "Because I believe that, particularly since the latter, particularly since let's say the FDR era in the 1930s, people have been consistently told to behave in ways that I consider financially irresponsible. And that is okay. That is fine. They don't need to be responsible because being responsible is the government's business…. So, I would consider that a form of modern day increasing immorality.

The lifestyle of you can have it now. See it, want it, charge it. You can have it all. As long as you have a pulse, you can qualify for a zero down mortgage, so get the biggest McMansion they make and put it on, not just a zero amortization, but even nowadays a negative amortization mortgage, where your monthly payment pays so little that your mortgage amount increases each month…. And the related reliance that, oh well, it is no big deal, so what if it all blows up and the housing bubble bursts and I am upside down in the mortgage and lose my house. No big deal because the government is always there. And, worst comes to worst, the government will bail me out, so I have nothing to worry about…. I mean what the heck, just have government provide the service and stick the next generation with the bill."

New Lifestyles and the Decline of Social Standards

Respondents frequently discussed the decline in social standards and families and the loss of respect for established institutions. Respondents reported on this loss of accepted social standards in different ways. This was manifested in things as small as cell phones ringing in restaurants or late night comedians making fun of leaders, priests or nuns. The loss of standards with respect to these small things was reflective of the overall loss of respect for social, religious and government institutions.

Respondents linked a social environment that lacked common values and standards with the loss of role models.

One person noted, "I used to feel, you know, as a kid growing up that adults were somebody I could look up to and have some security in, that they were stable, they had reached a point in their lives where they knew who they were and what they wanted and they were going to take care of the families, and it was just a purity. But now I see people who are depressed..."

Many respondents found the degradation and loss of standards in conduct indicative of a breakdown in society. Another respondent noted, "I just think we are becoming a nation where everybody is just ... you know, they do what they want. They view pornography and it has become an okay thing...And I don't--I don't think that is right. When you are seeing cuss words and stuff on TV in prime time and then the -- everybody thinks that is acceptable. I don't think that is acceptable."

New Lifestyles and Individualism

While some respondents were narrow in their interpretation of this question, and others perplexed by its ambiguity, many respondents identified new lifestyles with general values related issues such as materialism, selfishness, and a lack of adherence to moral and social standards. This characterization of lifestyles by some respondents matches fairly closely the description of the "lifestyle enclave" identified in *Habits of the Heart* (Bellah et al. 1985).

Habits of the Heart describes the lifestyle enclave as an expression of private life, linked closely with leisure and consumption. The life style enclave is typically unrelated to the world of work and "brings together those who are socially, economically, or culturally similar...one of its chief aims is the enjoyment of being with those who share one's lifestyle."

They note that lifestyle enclaves are based on a degree of

individual choice that is mostly independent from traditional ethnic and religious boundaries. "Whereas a community attempts to be an inclusive whole, celebrating the interdependence of public and private life and of the different callings of all, lifestyle is fundamentally segmental and celebrates the narcissism of similarity" (Bellah et al. 1985).

Besides measuring an individual's posture towards relativism and moral standards, this question also appeared to measure an important dimension of individualism and attitudes towards freedom. It tapped attitudes towards an "expressive individualism" that seeks to allow an autonomous self the freedom to select the values and lifestyle that maximize its own personal good. Expressive individualism seeks to allow each individual to define themselves and their own good. What may be lost in this expression of individual good is any sense of the common values, goals and good that must ultimately exist if people are to live in and maintain a society. Alexis de Tocqueville noted the dark side of this individualism which "disposes each citizen to isolate himself from the mass of his fellows and withdraw into his own circle of family and friends; with this little society formed to his taste, he gladly leaves greater society to look after itself" (De Tocqueville 1969).

New Lifestyles and the "Plentyplaint"

The lifestyles question appeared to tap some key moral beliefs. Following the 2004 election, many pundits were surprised by polls that showed that a high percentage of the electorate cited values as the more important factor in determining their vote choice. In his book after the election, Thomas Frank blames a conservative backlash movement driven by cultural issues. He describes voters who are more motivated by cultural issues than economic and class issues. He notes, "But the culture—the everyday environment they lived in —- rankled them the way pollen affects someone with hay fever. Their favorite magazines, movie heroes, and politicians would never let them forget it, either, parading before them an ever swelling cavalcade of grievances: tales of foul mouthed kids, crime in the streets, rabid feminists, out-of-control government agencies, crazy civil rights leaders, obscene art, welfare cheats, foolish professors, and sitcom provocations, each one sending them into swamps of bitterness" (Frank 2005, 141).

Frank argues that blue collar voters who are part of the conservative backlash movement have foolishly become captivated by cultural issues at the expense of their real economic interests. The answers of respondents to the lifestyles question were driven by cultural and values concerns. Similar to Frank's description of the conservative litany of complaints – what he calls the "plenty-plaint" – respondents did often describe their dissatisfaction with the new lifestyles as a list of the many small grievances.

These respondents would frequently link their many small concerns with society together with larger moral considerations. The way respondents would jump from small cultural concerns to larger values issues was reminiscent of the "broken windows" theory of the sociological origins of crime. The broken windows theory argues that small signs of the breakdown of order, such as a broken window on a house, cause greater disorder and criminal activity. Broken windows, graffiti, other small signs of neglect communicate to criminals that nobody cares. These superficial details in the social environment can actually serve to create a general atmosphere of lawlessness that encourages worse crimes. Respondent's description of the danger of "new lifestyles" often evoked the danger that relatively small changes in social habits, such as cuss words on television, or styles of dress, could have larger social implications.

There were a number of different ways in which respondents were conflicted about this question. A significant percentage of respondents did identify considerations both for and against this question. Concerns about the decay of society conflicted with the desire for personal freedom. Narrow interpretation of the question also caused some conflicts. Some who were supportive of gay rights disagreed with this question even though they made other comments that were indicative of concern about changes in moral beliefs in society. While this question was strongly associated with gay rights, a significant portion of respondents considered the question to be about broader overarching moral issues.

The question prompted some respondents to discuss different conceptions of what freedom should be used for. Unfettered freedom wasn't desirable when it eroded social standards, and led to violations of common standards of decency. Pornography, drug use, hedonism, excessive individualism and lack of respect for social standards were thought to be the result of new lifestyles by some.

Should We Adjust Our View of Moral Behavior to Changes in the World?

One of the questions that measures tolerance and moral traditionalism asks individuals to respond to the following statement: "The world is always changing and we should adjust our view of moral behavior to those changes." Overall, most respondents believed that you should be able to adjust your view of moral behavior based on changes in society, with 68 percent (19/28) either agreeing or agreeing strongly with this statement. None of the respondents expressed any overt ambivalence when choosing between these options. In general, respondents did not tend to discuss considerations on both sides of this question, with only 14 percent (4/28) discussing considerations both for and against the statement while answering. Partisanship did not appear to play a major role in framing this question, with only 4 percent (1/28) of respondents referring to the President, the administration or political parties. Respondents did frequently discuss issues of the day, with 75 percent (21/28) respondents mentioning such topics. Issues of the day would include policy or political issues that one might read about in a typical newspaper article. For instance, if one referred to gay marriage or stem cell research, this would be an issue of the day. If one just talked generally about one's belief in religion, then it would not be.

While the question was fairly vague, respondents did not express much confusion over how to interpret it. Only 14 percent (4/28) respondents made any reference to uncertainty about the meaning of the question. A number of respondents did note that it could be interpreted in different ways, but they then easily provided an interpretation that they had decided to use. This was not counted as confusion. Perhaps because the question refers to changes in the world, terrorism was mentioned in 32 percent (9/28) of the answers. It was also common for respondents to refer to gay marriage, gay adoption or other gay rights issue, with 50 percent (14/28) respondents referring to such issues. Respondents had a number of different interpretations and reactions to the question. These are discussed below in more detail.

Changes in the World

Respondents referred to a variety of different changes in the world that they thought might require adjustments in moral behavior. Terrorism was frequently cited. One respondent noted that it was justified for the U.S. to become more militant in the face of terrorist attacks. Changes in the world were also frequently interpreted to include the rise and fall of nations, changes in global markets and technological advances. The most common social issue referred to was gay rights, but issues related to racism and sexism were also discussed.

Changes in Our View of Moral Behavior

Respondents conceptualized changes in moral behavior in different ways as well. Respondents frequently blurred issues of personal morality with larger international issues. Respondents were asked to discuss what changes in moral behavior they thought of. One noted, "There it would tend to be more of how one treats other people and other governments, and I don't think we should change that."

Individuals frequently referred to changes in beliefs about the morality of homosexuality. One noted, "For example, homosexuality…in the old days it was condemned, but nowadays I think that people realize that we should have compassion for others, just because people thought one way many, many years ago doesn't mean that that is the right way to think…"

Respondents usually provided a reason why they thought morality should or should not change. A number of individuals discussed the benefits of tolerance. Some discussed relativism and their general lack of belief in the existence of morality, while others referred to religion and the existence of eternal and unchanging moral principles.

What is Morality?

A number of respondents were skeptical of defining moral beliefs. They saw reference to morality as a tool of those who were intolerant. One noted, "And I think we should adjust our moral -- I mean, what is morality anyway? You know, I always hear moral values. What does that mean, moral values? Does that mean biblical values? Does that mean-- I don't know what that means. It means nothing to me, you know....But I think that we need to -- we need to accept people, we need to, you know, accept what's happening instead of denying it and saying it's ungodly, or unbiblical, or whatever the Christian right is, you know, saying...."

There is No Single Standard of Morality

Individuals often defined tolerance as the most important value because they did not believe our society could have a single standard of morality. They were afraid to emphasize other aspects of morality because a single moral standard would be oppressive in a society as diverse as ours. "I just think to me it means treating other people with respect, respecting other people's ideas, their beliefs, their values. I don't think that there is a single standard of morality in this country, there can't be. We're too diverse ..."

Most respondents had a very flexible understanding of what morality was. One noted, "there are very few things that morally you can say are just black and white...there are some -- like killing people I think is bad, in terms of the way you dress or whether you decide to have one child or four children, those are things that are going to change -- our mind is changing, our collective mind as a culture and as a world is changing all the time."

Personal Freedom

A number of respondents argued that too much emphasis on moral values was a danger to personal freedom. Everybody should be allowed to "do their own thing" as long as they didn't force it upon other people. One woman noted, "I think he who has no sin should cast the first stone, because people who are kind of trying to be too moral, and trying to give people too many rules about morality and this that and the other, are kind of overstepping their bounds…really, once again, overstepping their bounds, most of the people I know don't care for people trying to give them the moral riot act…as I say, most people I know are not even doing anything that constitutes immorality, but someone else just takes it that way…they really just want to tell people what to do"

Technology Doesn't Change Moral Standards

While a number of individuals referred to changing technology as a key reason that morality needed to change, one woman argued that human nature, and the definition of morality, did not change fundamentally over time. She noted, "Because the world isn't changing that much that personal accountability and reactions are changing. I mean, we're still the same human beings that we were 50 years ago, it's just we now have TVs and cell phones. I don't -- I don't think anything should be adjusted. People should be more moral than they are but that doesn't mean we should change the definition."

The Need for Eternal Principles

In many of the answers, respondents who applied similar qualifications, or referred to similar examples, drew different conclusions. It seemed like individuals did not reason their way through to an answer, but rather, had a basic pre-disposition. Some people liked the idea of believing in absolute principles, while others found the notion distasteful. Religious beliefs often served as the basis for belief in absolute moral principles. A college student noted the following, "Number one, I am a born again evangelical Christian so I

don't really subscribe to moral relativism. So that is -- that's
my own rationale. But from a secular point of view it's like at
the end -- if we just put the peg in whatever hole at any time
then at the end of the day what do we hang our hat on -- hang
our hat on to believe in, you know what I mean? Like what
do you -- what are you going to look to? ..You might believe
in the all encompassing power of nature as a law of the
universe. And I'm like, yeah, that's great. Then live your life
according to that dictate. But if you don't have something at
the end of day, what has your life been? ...your life is kind of
meaningless if you don't believe in anything as an eternal
thing."

Religion Provides a Foundation for Absolute Moral Beliefs

Respondents who referred directly to their religious
beliefs were typically the ones that were willing to accept the
idea of absolute moral standards. "I think there are moral
absolutes. I think the modern idea of relativism, everything --
nothing is either right or wrong, it's the lens you view the
world through…For some things that's true, for issues of
morals it's usually not…. Issues of morals, that's another
story. And something is either moral or not, and that comes
from the fact that I'm a religious person anyway. And so
obviously, you know, you can't be religious and not have
some sort of set view of morals."

Some Morality is Absolute and Some is Not

Some respondents noted that it was ok for some moral
beliefs to change, but that there were core beliefs that could
not. Perhaps it was ok for society to be more lax about cuss
words on television, but just because sex crimes or rape

became more common did not mean that these things should be accepted. The balance between what should and should not be accepted was often difficult to strike. One did not want to be inflexible, but on the other hand, moral issues often had implications that went beyond the individual. One respondent noted,

"You know, that Victoria's Secret display they had at Tyson's Corner that was on the news. Maybe that's a good example….So they had very scantily dressed mannequins in very suggestive positions in their window and it was right next to a movie theater where a lot of kids go, and some people felt that it was not something appropriate for kids to see….So, you know, on the one hand I think we've become a freer society and, you know, people do dress more provocatively than they may have in the 18th century and it's more accepted, but on the other hand is this the image that we want to project to our children? I don't think so. So I think that while morally in some arenas the morals have been relaxed but in other arenas I think they need to be kept tighter."

Become Enlightened, but Don't Reshuffle the Moral Deck

One respondent, who neither agreed nor disagreed with the statement, also took a nuanced position. Human beings had become more enlightened on a variety of moral issues over time. Although this was a good thing, this did not imply that radical or wholesale changes to moral codes should be contemplated. Because human nature was unchanging, some moral standards were also not amenable to change.

"Because I think human nature has remained the same from the beginning of time. Like humans are greedy, scared, are hopeful, are stupid, are smart. I think that won't change. But at the same time our sensibilities are going to have to change on the issues. We have seen a drastic change, women can vote now, blacks can vote. You know, it's not appropriate to have children serving in the Army or working in factories…So, I mean, I think we've become enlightened on certain issues and we should account for that, but in the end human nature is what it is…. I do not necessarily think that it means we should precipitate some sort of full scale reshuffling of, you know, moral standards."

Reinterpret Morality to Apply to New Issues

A couple respondents argued that it was ok to adjust morality to account for new and unanticipated situations that were encountered in the world. Moral beliefs could remain relatively unchanged, but like the law, some adjudication of these standards was required to make them fit the many and diverse specific cases that one encountered.

"Because undeniably the world is changing in some respects. And even if we want to maintain a consistent moral standard, it is inevitably going to have to be reinterpreted and reapplied to confront new issues…. Because society is not going to remain static, we can't simply have a cookbook list of dos and don'ts and apply them in a computer-like fashion."

Scientific Knowledge and Morality

For one individual, advances in scientific knowledge required morality to be reinterpreted. They noted, "Because we need to adapt to changes in the situation in the world. Morality is close to absolute, but not absolute. People learn more and more about things that affect our moral choices. And moral choices become more and more complex. The Terry Schiavo thing, for example….And we have to use what we have learned to make appropriate moral choices in light of a changing world…Well, I mean there are some absolutes or close to absolutes. You know, perhaps using the Terry Schiavo case as an example, it perhaps wouldn't have been appropriate to remove her feeding tube, you know, ten years ago when she first fell into a vegetative state. We certainly don't understand everything about that state. And it would have been morally wrong to guess that she was never going to come out of that….I don't know all the ins and outs of things like partial-birth abortion, but certainly very late term abortions are on shaky moral ground, in my opinion…But, you know, an abortion at the stage of a four stage…four cell embryo is not."

Scientific knowledge also cast insight on the origins of human characteristics and behavior. With advances in genetic knowledge, behavior that was once considered a matter of free choice, or environmental conditioning, might come to be seen as deriving from a biological basis. As a result, behaviors that were once considered immoral might be reassessed in light of new information on the genetic bases of human behavior. Expanding on his statement above, the respondent noted, "Well, understanding complex issues. I am gay. And we are -- there is more and more evidence that that is not a choice I made, I was born that way…And that I think then has implications in terms of issues like gay marriage, equal rights for gays, you know, partner benefits and so forth. …We have learned -- science -- I am also a scientist and science is beginning to show us that -- that, you know, you are either born gay or you are not. And laws and morality need to adapt to that."

This question appears to measure one's basic posture towards tolerance and relativism. To the extent that the question asks respondents to choose between relativism and absolute moral standards, it may offer them a false choice. The moral considerations of most people are probably not based on such a false dichotomy. In *The Moral Sense*, James Q. Wilson argues that most people are, in fact, more sophisticated in their moral beliefs. He notes, "Someone once remarked that the two great errors in moral philosophy are the belief that we know the truth and the belief that there is no truth to be known. Only people who have had the benefit of higher education seemed inclined to fall into so false a choice. Ordinary people do not make this mistake. They believe they can judge human actions, albeit with great difficulty, and they believe that most disinterested people will make judgments that, if not identical, appeal to some shared sentiments. They are dismayed both by the claim that somebody is in the possession of absolute truth about all moral issues and by the thought that somebody thinks that there is no truth at all about them" (Wilson 1993).

Ambivalence in response to this question is perhaps not unexpected, given the moral choice it offers respondents. Respondents frequently qualified their answers, arguing both for absolute moral standards, and also for flexibility and nuance in the application of these standards.

Many respondents discussed gay rights when they answered this question, but it was not my impression that they considered this question to be primarily about gay rights. Rather, gay rights are an issue where the value of tolerance is often applied in our society today. When individuals reached for examples, it was easily accessible to them.

Should We Be More Tolerant of People Who Choose To Live According to Their Own Moral Standard?

The last question on moral traditionalism asked respondents to agree or disagree with the following statement: "We should be more tolerant of people who choose to live according to their own moral standards, even if they are very different from our own."

Tolerance is a first moral principle in our society, and 89 percent (25/28) of the respondents interviewed agreed or agreed strongly with this statement. Respondents were not ambivalent about this question, with none of them directly expressing their inability to answer because of conflicting strong emotions. Respondents were asked what they specifically could and could not tolerate, and 39 percent (11/28) respondents expressed considerations both for and against tolerance. Only 7 percent (2/28) of respondents made a direct reference to partisanship by referring to political parties, the administration or the president. Everyone seemed to understand what this question meant, and only 4 percent (1/28) respondents expressed any confusion over the question.

Many respondents referenced issues of the day, such as gay marriage, prayer in schools and abortion, with 46 percent (13/28) referring to these or other issues. It was very common for respondents to refer to gays when they answered this question, and 50 percent (14/28) did so.

Respondents had a range of interpretations and responses to this question. Some saw tolerance primarily through the lens of personal freedom. The tolerance of others was a precondition of having your own freedom respected. Some saw tolerance to mean that we should celebrate, embrace or love the differences that we encountered in others. Other respondents interpreted tolerance to mean only that we should put up with them, not persecute them, or try to change them.

Harm to Others

A very common reference point for answering this question was the harm to others principle. Of those interviewed, 57 percent (16/28) made reference to the idea that anything that didn't harm others should be tolerated. The harm to others principle was expressed in different ways. In a number of cases, harm to others was considered to be any infringement on the rights of others. One respondent noted, "I think everyone should be able to do pretty much and live pretty much how they want to as long as they're not infringing on someone else's rights to do the same thing." This question was importantly related to the value of freedom, and many respondents referred directly to freedom when they answered. One said, "I believe in the live and let live. As long as -- as long as it doesn't hurt me or mine, you know, it's free choice." Respondents varied in the extent that they saw specific behaviors as affecting others. Some considered only direct harm, while others also made reference to behaviors that "affected others". Actions that didn't affect others were "nobody's business". For some respondents, drug use was ok, and could be tolerated, while for others, it could not. The use of the harm to others principle was common, but individuals often considered different types of actions to be appropriate or not, depending on how big a footprint they saw individual behavior having on other social relations.

Diversity

One argument for tolerance that came up frequently was that the diversity of our society made it necessary. Many respondents also linked tolerance to individualism and freedom. To live in a free and diverse society, tolerance was necessary. One respondent noted, "Everyone has different personal experiences, everyone has different backgrounds, everyone has different beliefs …I mean, we're not going to have the same education or the same views just because you're an individual. I think that's what's special about our population. We're not all robots where we have the same information or same views. They're all different and they're all distinctive."

Similarity: All Moralities Have the Same Principles

Another respondent argued that tolerance was possible because of the similarities between individuals. It was actually the fact that all major moralities had similar moral principles that made tolerance feasible. In the consideration of moral views, one was unlikely to encounter a completely alien moral philosophy. He noted, "most of the religions of the world provide a body of moral standards and if you look at them they're all pretty much the same, you know, but some go to church, some go to a mosque, some go to a temple, some go to meditate, okay. ...I guess I see a lot more commonality in the world and I focus on the commonality rather than the differences, and if people really -- and if other people, more people focused what we have in common and respect other ways of -- other people's ways of doing things, this world would be a hell of a lot better off."

What is More Tolerant?

Individuals defined more tolerant in different ways. Some discussed tolerance in the context of behaviors that one would find distasteful, but nonetheless be required to endure. One noted, "if somebody is standing over there completely naked, you don't have to look at them…that's tolerating them…someone is over there, they're walking around with a skinhead, and they say they are a Nazi, and they say everyone else should go away that doesn't look like him, you have to tolerate that, as long as it does not cross over the line to hate"

People often discussed typical vices as things that should be tolerated. Drug use, pornography, drunkenness and other bad habits were often mentioned. Typically respondents modified these expressions of tolerance with the harm to others principle. One noted, "People who like pornography, as long as …no one is being physically injured, there is a line in the sand, of course for people who enjoy pornography, as long as what they are viewing is not of someone being physically abused, or someone under an age where they cannot give consent for that to occur."

For some, tolerance implied that one would be required to live with things that they knew were wrong. Explaining tolerance, one individual said, "Saying, okay, yeah, you know it ain't right but I -- I can live with that. You know, you've got your own thing. I'm just going to allow it because we're supposed to – we're not supposed to cast judgment on nobody, you know"

For some individuals, tolerance was the means to achieve a greater good. It might be distasteful in some circumstances and it wouldn't always be easy to live with. One individual summed up tolerance by noting, "We have all sorts of nonsense…but that's the cost of freedom." Another said, "Just accepting it without making a stink over it. You know, if your neighbors are doing something that you don't like you just wouldn't say anything about it. That's I guess what more tolerant means." This version of tolerance was usually summed up by statements such as "live and let live" or "we may disagree, but we can accept".

There seemed to be a fairly wide spectrum of belief about what tolerance implied. Thus while for some tolerance meant that you would merely stay out of other people's affairs, and generally ignore them, other respondents believed that tolerance required a more active stance. Those with stronger religious beliefs often mentioned the idea that you should still love those who you disagreed with. One individual noted the following, "Accepting people for who they are, loving them in spite of what they are whether you agree with them or not. I don't agree with the gay lifestyle but I still love the people who are gay."

For some, tolerance required that one be moderate and less absolute in one's own beliefs. For them, tolerance implied flexibility in the way one conceptualized the moral universe.

To be tolerant, one could not always believe that they knew what was right. One respondent said, "Like being able to accept and adjust to other people's views, not believing that your way is the right way -- not that it's not the right way but -- not believing that your way is the only way and acting or behaving in a way where, you show belief – that your view in life should be explored by everyone else. That's not the way it is."

Perhaps somewhat further along the tolerance scale was the belief that tolerance should include respect for other people. For some, tolerance was an expression of respect for the individuality of others. One person said, "I just think that we need to have a general level of respect for other people. I think that – it's like going back to the homosexuality thing. I'm not homosexual but, if I were, the thought of somebody telling me who to love or who I can or can't love or have a relationship with really offends me and I think that that's wrong. I just don't think that we have a right to do that."

A little further along the spectrum of beliefs about tolerance was the view of some that tolerance implied that we should integrate those who are different into our lives. Some respondents argued that tolerance meant that we should be friends with those who are different, and we should not try to convert them to our way. One respondent said that tolerance meant the following, "Less judgmental, more accepting. Like being friends with someone who's Jewish if you're Christian or being friends with someone who's an Atheist if you're Jewish or whatever. Or like -- I think it also includes an element of not being evangelist, of not -- if you -- if you are a devout Christian like not saying, Ah, nice to meet you. Have you accepted Jesus into your heart yet? You know what I mean?"

Perhaps furthest along the spectrum of tolerance were those that saw tolerance as requiring the active affirmation of the beliefs of others. One respondent noted, "I think we should celebrate each other." To some extent the beliefs about tolerance expressed interpretations of what the object of tolerance was. For instance, nobody expressed the belief that we should celebrate pornographers.

On the other hand, the topics individuals chose to talk about were probably related to their general predisposition towards tolerance. Those who were most favorably disposed towards tolerating others chose to discuss it in the context of friendships with others. Those who were not may have chosen to see tolerance as being something that was less enjoyable.

Diversity and Intolerance of Mainstream Beliefs

When questions of religion were involved, it was often difficult to define what tolerance was. Policies to encourage diversity and tolerance were sometimes seen as intolerant of mainstream religious beliefs. One respondent noted the following, "And I think there is a real hypocrisy here on the part of the liberal elite in this country -- and it seeps into education in a really weird way. Everybody is look, oh, tolerance, and diversity and all that good stuff, global community, it takes a village to raise a child and all that shit, but then I think in the mainstream press, academia and in the legal community there is severe bias against Christians -- I get almost apoplectic about it because it's just such a blatant hypocrisy. Like with the ACLU, they will say -- say a teacher wears a cross necklace to school. I mean, this happened in Pittsburgh. They will run to that school to try and get that teacher removed or take that necklace off or whatever.

But in California recently a group of concerned parents who happened to be Christians sued a school, which I'm not saying is right, sued a school for having a classroom demonstration, and it was to educate them about Islam. It was race to Mecca and doing all this stuff to educate them about Islam....Now where was the ACLU on that one? They were nowhere to be found. Say if it was a thing that emphasized Christianity – if it was all about Christianity, they would be beating down the door. And that is the kind of moral hypocrisy that really rubs me the wrong way."

Freedom – It's Best When We Make Our Own Decisions

A common frame of reference for discussing tolerance was personal freedom. Because it is often the case that it is impossible to define what moral goods a person should want, tolerance and freedom are necessary to allow each individual to pursue a moral life. One respondent said, "I have no right to tell someone how to live their life. I definitely have no insight into what it means to be them and...so given that they're probably the best person to make the decision for themselves, I think we should -- people should be left alone to do what's good for them as long as they're not hurting anyone -- they can even hurt themselves to a certain extent I think."

The importance of freedom to make moral choices was discussed in religious terms by some. One respondent noted, "I think that each person has to be convinced in his own heart of what's right and wrong and the only thing that can convince a person is the Holy Spirit. We can -- we can try to tell them what's right or wrong, but most times we'll push people away if we try to tell them"

For some, the importance of tolerance is that we usually lack the knowledge of what is best for other people. "Because I think none of us has the wisdom to serve as an effective judge of others. And that if we attempt to take on that role, it is a role we are not qualified for…I think we have all we can do and then some to see to it that our own individual lives are run as best we can."

While some might define self-destructive practices, such as "dope use, alcohol use, the use of fried and fatty foods" as immoral, the freedom to make choices was a prerequisite to being a moral person. One respondent noted, "People should be free to go to Hell in their own way".

Things That You Don't Agree With, but Should Be Tolerated

Respondents were asked to discuss moral views that they might not agree with, but could still be tolerated. Some respondents had a difficult time describing practices that they didn't agree with. The value of tolerance was so strong in many people that they hesitated to identify things that they disagreed with. One respondent noted, "I'm a pretty open minded guy…there's not a whole lot that offends me in terms of what people do with themselves….Oh, I don't know, maybe, cross dressing. I think it's nothing I'm interested in but I think definitely -- it should be tolerated, or people that are trans-gender. It's nothing -- I can't get my head around what that means, but if someone legitimately feels that they're stuck in the wrong body I think they should be able to correct that situation".

Is There Anything That We Can't Tolerate?

Respondents were asked if there is anything that we should not tolerate. In general, people reached for heinous crimes, such as child molestation and child abuse.

"So I think we need to be tolerant to a point. If somebody believes that it's not immoral to have sex with children, well, I'm not going to condone that and I'm not going to accept that."

While respondents were often hesitant to apply moral standards, it was in the case of children where they often drew the line most starkly. One noted, "If you've got a child molester…I'm not going to allow that, it doesn't matter what kind of crazy system they come from or what sort of morals they have." Another noted that one could not tolerate "beating your kids or locking them in a box."

Intolerance of Violating the Golden Rule

Respondents weren't asked to discuss whether intolerance should be tolerated. Interestingly, one of the few respondents who answered that we should not be more tolerant towards others argued that it was necessary to be intolerant of those that didn't respect the rights of others.

"I disagree because when I think of morals, I think it's a simple, everyday thing…you treat people the way you want to be treated and you don't cheat, lie or steal kind of thing. I mean, no, I'm not going to be cool with somebody with loose morals, just because they want to have loose morals like that, that kind of thing…. It means relaxing my own standards for myself, I'm not going to be more tolerant of obnoxious people….you could look out this window and see people cutting each other off in traffic -- I just feel like it's obnoxious….people need to be less self-centered. I'm not going to be more tolerant of them being more self-centered."

Tolerance is a dominant value in our society. It was difficult for respondents to disagree with a statement saying we should be more tolerant. There was a wide variance in how respondents defined tolerance, suggesting that this question does not capture the diversity of beliefs that respondents actually held concerning tolerance. This is consistent with the findings of some scholars who have argued that the measurement of tolerance is crucially related to the target of tolerance being considered (Sullivan, Pierson and Marcus 1979). While most respondents endorsed the value of tolerance, some orthodox respondents were concerned that the spread of relativism in education, governmental policies and laws was intolerant of core Christian values. Similar to Hunter's thesis, the debate over tolerance was not so much concerned with whether society should be tolerant, but how to define tolerance.

Many respondents referenced freedom when they answered this question, indicating that it may also be a good measure of the value of freedom. The question tapped important libertarian beliefs regarding freedom, and it was very common for individuals to refer to the "harm to others" principle when discussing the statement.

Previous studies have found that the value of tolerance is often held more strongly by individuals that are exposed to a more diverse social environment. Psychological research on opinions and beliefs has suggested that "People adopt opinions not only to understand the world, but also to meet the psychological and social needs to live with themselves and others" (Jervis 2006). In this sense, the value of tolerance is a useful belief to hold for those that are exposed to a more diverse society.

Gay marriage and gay rights were discussed by about half of the respondents. While this question was often related to gay issues, I didn't get the impression that respondents saw the question as a proxy for opinions about gay rights.

Conclusions

Given the opportunity, respondents frequently qualified their answers to questions measuring moral traditionalism. While some respondents could be classified as relativists or moral absolutists, the vast majority of respondents were more nuanced and ambivalent in their responses to these questions. Many experienced conflicts between moral traditionalism and freedom. The questions receiving the greatest levels of support were those moral values questions where personal freedom reinforced the moral view. For instance, the high levels of support for moral tolerance were directly tied to considerations of individual freedom for many.

Both issues of gay rights and larger moral considerations were discussed under all of the questions measuring moral traditionalism. Some scholars have argued that the NES questions asking about emphasis on traditional family ties and the role of new lifestyles tap a separate family values construct (Layman 2005). My interviews found discussion of both family values and more general issues of moral orthodoxy under all four of the NES questions measuring moral considerations.

Respondents brought in a wide array of considerations and interpretations for each of the questions. For instance, widespread agreement on the value of tolerance masked large underlying differences in what individuals thought this question meant. In many cases, respondents showed a willingness to take absolute moral stands on some issues, while also expressing the need for moral flexibility in other cases. Many expressed a fear of moral decay, and distaste for the loss of freedom that could result from excessive moralism.

To the extent that individuals tended to be divided within themselves, these results confirm Wolf's thesis of a lack of stark division and polarization between individuals (Wolf 1999). Many respondents had the ability to identify positive and negative considerations on both sides of a given moral question. On the other hand, respondents did tend to define tolerance, morality and the family in significantly different ways when they answered. Their arguments for and against different definitions of these values were like ships passing in the night. In this sense, these results lend some credence to Hunter's idea of deep seated cultural differences between world views (Hunter 1991).

While Hunter posited that progressives and the orthodox defined freedom in different ways, most respondents tended to view freedom in negative terms, as a lack of restraint on individual behavior. Some respondents did articulate a belief that people should not be free to do anything, but no one articulated what would be considered a fully fleshed out concept of positive freedom. Perhaps this is because this is a somewhat difficult concept to fully convey in a short conversation.

Respondents linked issues together in diverse and unpredictable ways. Unlike Hunter's thesis of an isomorphism between moral and other policy dimensions, systematic linkages between morals and other policies were not immediately evident. For instance, while Hunter postulates a linkage between orthodoxy and militarism, many respondents made the opposite linkage, arguing that changes in the world, the attacks of September 11 specifically, justified some moral flexibility and a shift away from pacifism.

Hunter postulated a linkage between progressive moral beliefs and support for the welfare state. At least within my sample, the issues were not clearly linked together. There were strong libertarians who combined a strong anti-government sentiment with an equally strong attachment to personal freedom from moral dictates. There were fundamentalists who were strong advocates of extensive wealth redistribution.

Layman has argued that conflict extension characterizes the division within the electorate over moral issues (Layman and Carsey 2002). According to him, moral beliefs are not a cross-cutting issue, eclipsing old dimensions of political conflict. Rather, the new moral divide has been super-imposed onto the old political divisions and has served to extend the issues over which partisans are divided. Instead of defining a new political universe, cultural issues have just served to further divide highly aware activists who perceive party differences on specific issues.

It is difficult to speak directly to this with such a small sample, but highly aware individuals in my sample tended to hold unconventional libertarian combinations of beliefs that were not easily translated into a Republican-Democratic

partisan issue divide. In addition, strong partisan beliefs were
not that common. Respondents openly admitted to not
voting, not being interested in politics or believing that "both
parties stink." It is likely that my interview sample was too
small to include many political activists. On the other hand,
these results reinforce the findings of most scholars that
political activist and partisan ideologues comprise only a
small share of the electorate.

As you might expect, those holding progressive beliefs
tended to be more ambivalent than the orthodox. Not being
strongly attached to absolute moral principles, they more
often sought to qualify their answers to provide more flexible
and nuanced responses.

While some political scientists have sought to define
public beliefs as lacking substance (Zaller 1992; Converse
1964), my overall impression of respondents was more
positive. They might be conflicted in expressing their values,
but most respondents did seem to discuss their core beliefs in
a very personal and deeply felt manner. The set of ideas they
put forward might lack a sharp ideological clarity, but they
seemed to embody balanced consideration of the values
questions. At least in my sample, respondents were
inconsistent in their answers, not because they didn't care, but
because they were conflicted in their values. They understood
values issues to be complex, and not easily reducible to yes or
no answers. They saw issues as involving difficult moral
tradeoffs that were not easy to make. Unlike some scholars
(Alvarez and Brehm 2002) who have argued that true
ambivalence is rare, these results suggest that the public is
conflicted on a fairly wide range of moral issues.

These findings are interesting because they cast doubt, as
does much of the scholarly literature, on the idea that the
public has become polarized, and that political compromise is
impossible. Much of the public is conflicted, ambivalent and
open to the appeal of politicians who address the complexity
of their moral universe. To argue that the moral universe of

the public is complex is not to argue that the public does not care about moral issues. Respondents had real concerns about the moral climate of the country that were deeply felt.

One conclusion that could be drawn from these results is that politicians will be most successful when they advance moral libertarian agendas. Programs that serve to maximize individual freedom and tolerance, while also addressing moral concerns are likely to be most consistent with the public's values. For example, an education program focused on school choice is thus more consistent with the public's values than one that seeks to inject moral content into the public school system. The public wants to live in a tolerant society, but this also means a society that allows them to transmit the values they think are important to their children. The public's moral beliefs are a tapestry of different ideas and not easily reducible to a simple political divide. This type of complexity is best addressed through policies that maximize individual freedom.

Chapter 4: Measures of Equality

It is often said that equality is the first and most important American political value. On visiting America in 1830, De Tocqueville wrote that "equality of condition is the fundamental fact from which all others seem to be derived and the central point to which all my observations returned"(De Tocqueville 1969). Many scholars of modern public opinion would agree that the value of equality plays a crucial role in shaping American political attitudes (Feldman 1988; Feldman and Steenbergen 2001; Alvarez and Brehm 2002).

Despite the centrality and importance of equality in political culture, elites and the public at large, have often held conflicted and inconsistent beliefs about equality. Public opinion scholars have found that much of the public is ambivalent about economic equality (Hochschild 1981) and some aspects of racial equality (Hochschild 2006).

Students of public opinion have often argued that values are distinguished by their stability and durability in the public mind (Rokeach 1973). In the National Election Studies Survey, public beliefs about equality have been shown to be significantly unstable (Feldman 1999). If equality is such a central value in American culture, what can be made of the inconsistencies and instability in public beliefs about the value of equality? How can the public care so much about equality and yet be so ambivalent? This chapter employs in-depth interviews to delineate what Americans believe about equality.

The Meaning of Equality

To study the value of equality, one must distinguish between the different meanings and interpretations of equality itself. In the public mind, equality has several different dimensions which can conflict with one another, including equality before the law, equality of opportunity and equality of outcome. Given current or historical inequities, providing the same legal rights to everyone may not be consistent with providing a level playing field and equal opportunity. Similarly, given naturally occurring differences in physical characteristics, intelligence and luck, providing equal opportunity will, by definition, lead to unequal outcomes. Conflicts between equality before the law, equal opportunity and equality of outcome have not been extensively studied by scholars due to the survey tools and questions available (Feldman 1999). The interviews described in this chapter cast some light on how respondents think about these and other dimensions of equality. A number of different research frameworks have been used by scholars to explain value conflicts in public opinion. These are briefly described below.

Ambivalence

Scholars have put forward a number of different theories to explain public beliefs about equality. In her seminal study of equality in America, *What's Fair?*, Hochschild argued that Americans were fundamentally ambivalent in their beliefs about equality and fairness (1981). They often applied the value of equality differently in separate domains of their lives. While individuals generally endorsed the value of equality in their social and political lives, in the economic domain, they were conflicted about how equal things should be.

Hochschild believed that the public was incapable of

challenging the dominant free market ideology in the U.S. It was a lack of social imagination that prevented the public from demanding something better. Nonetheless, respondents were ambivalent in their views of economic equality, trapped between what they thought should be and their understanding of what was possible. Hochschild found the public's ambivalence toward equality to be notable because psychologists have traditionally argued that individuals seek to hold beliefs that are consistent. Individual's holding inconsistent values or beliefs experience cognitive dissonance (Festinger 1957). Cognitive dissonance is uncomfortable and individuals seek to adjust their beliefs over time to avoid this condition.

A somewhat different perspective on ambivalence is provided by the cognitive efficiency school of thought (Taylor 1981). Researchers have frequently noted that individuals do not collect exhaustive information about most things or seek to develop consistent sets of beliefs if there is no tangible benefit. In most cases, they can comfortably live with many inconsistent beliefs. It is only when inconsistent beliefs are made simultaneously accessible to them that they may experience cognitive dissonance. In a sense, Hochschild's interview process made subjects aware of the inconsistencies between their values and beliefs.

Differing Information Levels, Values and Reasoning

The amount of political information possessed by individuals has also been shown to be an important determinant of how individuals structure and use their values. For instance, one phenomenon some political scientists have struggled with is the principle-policy puzzle. Although most Americans strongly endorse the value of equality, they often do not endorse the specific policies to ensure equality. This puzzle can be explained by two different processes used to reason about policy issues related to equality. High information individuals tend to use conservative beliefs about limited government to modify the application of their abstract beliefs about equality (Sniderman, Brody and Tetlock 1991). Those with less information tend to use their feelings about specific groups, rather than their values, to determine their attitudes about specific policies to ensure equality.

In later work, Hochschild also noted how important feelings about, and membership in specific groups, were to the application of the value of equality. For instance, she argued that there is a black ambivalence about equality. Many blacks endorse policies to promote equality for blacks, but not for other racial groups. White ambivalence toward equality also existed. Many whites strongly endorsed the value of equality in the abstract, but not the policies that would help ensure equality, like reparations or policies against racial profiling (Hochschild 2006).

Alvarez and Brehm have argued that true ambivalence is rare (2002). In most cases, increasing levels of information tend to reduce value conflicts by allowing the public to more consistently connect their values to each other. The public is ambivalent about hard issues such as euthanasia and abortion, where greater levels of information are associated with greater levels of ambivalence. For these issues, the public is forced to choose between two incommensurable values and more information only makes the choice more stark, clearly drawn and difficult.

Framing

Issue framing is important because it determines what values the public uses when it forms an opinion. A number of scholars have noted that the public often hold holds contradictory values regarding equality, and which values are applied depends on whether the issue is discussed in a social or individualistic frame of reference. For instance, in their study of inequality, Kluegel and Smith (1986) found that the dominant American ideology consisted of three core individualistic beliefs. The public believed that opportunity for advancement was widespread, individuals were personally responsible for their positions and that therefore, social inequalities were more or less fair. Layered on top of these core individualistic beliefs were more liberal ideas about the importance of equality for all groups in society as a whole.

These two sets of beliefs existed on separate planes from each other. Public policies, such as job training, that appealed to both personal responsibility and to social liberalism were consistent with both values and tended to be the most popular. The public supported individualistic policies to achieve equality, but systemic solutions to remedy inequality were not consistent with the values of most of the public.

Other scholars have discovered similar findings. For instance, in a study of beliefs about the welfare state, Feldman and Zaller found that the public was philosophically conservative and operationally liberal (1992). The public endorsed personal responsibility and individualism, while also being for a range of government programs to address social needs. Those who endorsed the welfare state were conflicted between their desire for programs to alleviate inequality and their equally strong individualistic beliefs.

More recently Feldman (2003) has argued that public support for the Bush tax cuts can be explained by a similar schism between the public's beliefs about macro-justice and micro-justice. The public supports market mechanisms and reward for merit. When answering questions about individual salaries, the public believes that pay should be based on merit, not on need. At the same time, the public also believes that the overall distribution of income in society is unfair. At the macro-level, the public strongly endorses the principle of equality. Some scholars have argued that the public's attachment to market justice requires social reformers to re-conceptualize political justice in order to provide a popular ideological justification for egalitarian values (Lane 1986). In each of these cases, scholars have shown that the public holds individualistic beliefs related to equality of opportunity and a more general social understanding of equality which is tied to the idea of equality of outcome. This conflict within the value of equality itself affects beliefs about many specific issues.

Psychological Bases for Conflicting Beliefs about Equality of Opportunity

The foundation for ambivalence toward equality can also be found in psychological processes. Political psychologists have argued that individuals hold beliefs for a variety of reasons. One reason people hold beliefs is that they are useful for their survival. The principal of cognitive mastery states that people seek to understand their place in the world and they construct mental models that will help them guide their actions. People are attached to the idea that they are in control of their own fate because this is a useful idea. The belief in the importance of equal opportunity is associated with a belief in self-mastery. To the extent one believes that society provides equality of opportunity to all, one believes they are in control of their fate.

There are psychological benefits to believing that you can control your life. Belief in control over one's environment can help to motivate action. This will benefit the individual if indeed they can have some influence. Overall, "trying to act effectively in situations that are actually uncontrollable often carries little cost, compared to failing to act when it would be helpful…Overall effectiveness in dealing with the environment would be maximized by a tendency to overestimate one's ability to control or influence events…" (Kluegel and Smith 1986). Researchers have argued that humans are hard wired to overestimate their control over the environment.

In addition, the belief in your ability to control your fate can also have important psychological and health benefits. Even in animals "the ability to terminate electric shocks by pressing a lever reduces the harmful motivational, behavioral, and emotional consequences for rats compared to identical uncontrollable shocks" (Kluegel and Smith 1986). People who believe they are in control of their life function better from both a psychological and physiological perspective.

The belief that society should or does provide equal opportunity has powerful bases of support in individual psychology. The belief in meritocracy and a just world where individuals are rewarded based on their own efforts is part and parcel of the belief that one is in control of their own destiny. As a result, this is often an idea that individuals seek to protect, even if it means holding a set of beliefs that are inconsistent with each other.

The principle of cognitive efficiency is another reason why people are often attached to individualistic explanations for success or failure. Individuals often look for the most readily available and most easily identifiable causal factors to explain their world. Individual behavior is the most salient and readily available explanation for the causes of success or failure. Psychologists have called the bias of people toward individual explanations of behavior, and away from situational explanations, "the fundamental attribution error". The fundamental attribution error may explain why some people are strongly attracted to the idea that everyone does have an equal chance and that it is our actions that matter"(Kluegel and Smith 1986).

Self-esteem maintenance is another function that beliefs

serve. People seek to maintain their self-esteem through the use of defensive biases. For instance, individuals have the tendency to over-attribute positive outcomes to themselves, while locating the causes of negative outcomes in external factors. Robert Lane has argued that there is a fear of equality in society among the working class (Lane 1962). If one has a lower income, or is in danger of losing one's job and falling into poverty, there is a tendency to want to psychologically distance oneself from the poor as a defense mechanism. "Working class people need to distance themselves psychologically from the poor in order to maintain a favorable social identity and self-esteem…one way to do this is to emphasize the lack of moral character, effort, or talent on the part of the poor, in contrast to the more favorably viewed characteristics of the working class" (Kluegel and Smith 1986). Similarly, if one is poor, one's defense mechanism would tend to bias one towards systemic explanations for the cause of this.

Individuals thus may hold beliefs to satisfy certain social or psychological needs, and may in some cases hold conflicting beliefs for different reasons. Individuals are strongly attached to notions of individual control embodied in the idea that everyone has an equal chance. Ambivalence towards equality may be driven by multiple psychological needs that lead individuals to adopt, and simultaneously hold conflicting beliefs.

Data and Research Methods

This chapter utilizes in-depth interviews to understand how respondents interpret the meaning of the value of equality. Note that more detailed information on the selection and composition of the respondents interviewed, and the qualitative research methods used is provided in Chapter 2. The NES uses six different questions to measure the value of equality. Respondents were asked each of these questions, as well as numerous follow-up questions about why they answered the way they did and what different terms in the question meant to them. There are many dimensions of the value of equality, including equality before the law, equality of opportunity and equality of outcome. Most of the NES questions are more closely associated with equality of opportunity, although respondents' answers tended to refer to more than one of these dimensions and to blur the distinctions between the different dimensions of equality. Responses to some of these questions are described in more detail below.

Our Society Should Do Whatever Is Necessary to Make Sure That Everyone Has an Equal Opportunity to Succeed.

The first question dealt directly with equality of opportunity. Individuals were asked to respond to the following statement: "Our society should do whatever is necessary to make sure that everyone has an equal opportunity to succeed." Respondents could either agree, agree strongly, neither agree nor disagree, disagree or disagree strongly. Respondents overwhelmingly endorsed this statement. None of the respondents disagreed. Only 7 percent of the respondents (2/28) neither agreed nor disagreed. Approximately 61 percent (17/28) strongly agreed and 32 percent (9/28) agreed.

There was relatively little ambivalence associated with this question, with only 11 percent (3/28) respondents expressing conflicted strong feelings about their response. Discussing considerations both for and against the statement was more common, with 36 percent (10/28) of respondents doing this. While the results were somewhat homogeneous, with respondents overwhelmingly agreeing with the statement, there was some diversity in how individuals defined what equal opportunity meant. Individuals tended to define the question in the manner that allowed them to answer in the affirmative. Only one respondent expressed confusion over what the statement meant.

Mention of political parties, the President or the administration did not occur in the sample of people I spoke with, suggesting that it is not common for individuals to use a partisan frame of reference when answering this question. Reference to issues that one might read about in the daily newspaper was more common, with 64 percent (18/28) of respondents referring to "issues of the day". General references to education were common, and coding these as issues of the day raised the percentage considerably.

What Is Equal Opportunity?

Individuals defined equal opportunity in a variety of ways. For some, equal opportunity meant preventing discrimination. Closely associated with this idea was the notion that equal opportunity implied a meritocracy. A number of individuals discussed equal opportunity in individualistic terms. For them, equal opportunity was about empowering a self-reliant and hardworking individual.

In some cases, respondents thought equal opportunity also created certain types of inequality. Equal opportunity was the right of the individual to have an equal chance to be successful. Not everyone would win in this competition, and thus the social mobility that equal opportunity fostered would reward some more than others. While some respondents were individualistic in their conception of equal opportunity, other respondents were more egalitarian. For them, equal opportunity meant a more even distribution of resources. Many respondents mentioned education when discussing equal opportunity. Achieving social advancement through education was perhaps the most common understanding of what equal opportunity meant.

When respondents applied the value of equal opportunity to specific policy areas, they tended to come to different conclusions. For some, equal opportunity was associated with affirmative action programs. For others, affirmative action was the antithesis of equal opportunity. Respondents had trouble objecting to the value of equal opportunity. This overall level of agreement masked significant differences in what they thought equal opportunity was. The diversity of this response is discussed in more detail below.

Meritocracy

The concept of a meritocracy was invoked by a number of individuals. Developing standards of hiring or promotion based on merit was discussed both in the context of racial and ethnic differences, but it was also referred to by respondents who didn't mention these subjects. One respondent noted, "People of the same educational level and aptitude should have equal opportunity to advance in their profession, a level playing field." A number of respondents mentioned the role of work in achieving success. They argued, "Nobody should be denied the opportunity to succeed. If they're working their asses off ... then they're eligible for the opportunity for sure."

Equal opportunity did not imply that society should allocate resources and rewards to the individual and expect nothing in return. Indeed, respondents usually argued explicitly that providing equal opportunity was not a giveaway for the individual. One noted, "It is not handed to you on a silver platter. But the opportunity is available to you if you want to take it." Equal opportunity was viewed by respondents as being consistent with, and maybe even requiring, a strong individual. Equal opportunity provided the social framework for success, but it was the empowered self-reliant individual that was responsible for obtaining the results.

Social Mobility and the Possibility of Rising to the Top

Equal opportunity was often discussed in the context of the competition for the best jobs and leadership positions. The social mobility made possible by equal opportunity allowed some to rise on the economic or social latter. One respondent noted, "Well, if I wanted to be a lawyer, I should be able to pursue that. If I wanted to be a physician, I should be able to do that. I mean, that's what the American dream is. You should be able to ...become whatever you want to become -- president, you know...."

Equal opportunity created winners and losers in the social and economic arena. The right to succeed also allowed for the possibility of failure as well. One individual said, "It means an equal chance. It doesn't mean necessarily that everybody is going to be the CEO of every corporation. It just means you have that option."

Equal Opportunity and Resources

Some respondents framed the issue of equal opportunity in a more egalitarian fashion. These respondents tended to discuss this issue not in terms of legal or social barriers to advancement, but rather, they discussed the concrete resources that one would need to obtain opportunities. A quality education, access to good teachers, tax breaks and tax credits were mentioned by respondents. Some respondents discussed numerous resources that were necessary to achieve equality of opportunity. As the list of items needed to achieve equality of opportunity became longer, some respondents blended the concept of equality of opportunity with more general beliefs about the need to reduce the overall level of inequality in society.

Respondents frequently mentioned education when discussing equality of opportunity. Perhaps because education has become the basis for advancement in our society, it was also the most common reference point for talking about equality and opportunity. Many respondents discussed the lack of access to a quality education as the major barrier to equality of opportunity.

Equality of opportunity did not imply that everybody should have the same things or want the same things. There was no one single standard or single good that individuals were competing for. Rather, equality of opportunity allowed individuals the freedom to define their own good. It sought to minimize social barriers that block individuals from achieving their goals. Equality of opportunity thus required that maximum space be provided for individuals to exercise their freedom. One woman put it this way, "It just means being given a fair chance to be successful and to live your life in whatever way you see fit. I don't think that that means that everyone should be college educated. I don't think everyone is meant to go to college and or should even want to go to college. I don't think everyone is meant to have the same kind of career or job or station in life....But I just think that there should be opportunity for everyone to carve out their niche and do what they think is the best for their lives..."

Affirmative Action

A number of respondents did not believe that affirmative action was consistent with the value of equality of opportunity. One noted, "But I think in terms of things like race and gender and everything, everyone should have a completely equal opportunity....I don't agree with affirmative action. Everything should be based completely on merit, you know. The best man for the job." When asked what equality of opportunity was, one respondent noted, "I think the wording of the 1965 Civil Rights Amendments couldn't be beat. It says very clearly and plainly that housing and employment and other issues are not to be determined on the basis of race, creed, color, sex or place of national origin…It says that as clearly as humans could ever put something into English…And for that to have been reversed one hundred and eighty degrees so that, within a matter of a few years, the Supreme Court had ruled a law that says we absolutely must not discriminate really means that what we must do is discriminate in favor of the poor, disadvantaged people…To have reversed the clear meaning of the law to exactly its opposite within …I think it was maybe five, six years of the law being passed …Is to me, just a staggering example of why government is not to be trusted with power."

The only doubt that respondents displayed about equal opportunity was the phrasing of the statement that said society "should do whatever is necessary." The reference led some respondents who favored equal opportunity strongly to say they somewhat agreed. The absolute nature of this statement led some to consider that there might be other values that equality of opportunity would need to be balanced against.

An Impossible Ideal

A number of respondents noted that equality of opportunity was an ideal that was impossible to achieve in reality. It was impossible both because of the wide diversity of human personalities and circumstances, and also because of the limitations of government and society to remediate these differences.

One respondent noted, "Because although I strongly

endorse the idea of people having an equal opportunity to succeed, in the real world that is not ever going to be the case.... Some people are born smart, some are born stupid. Some are born healthy, some are born sick.... And for government to attempt to redress the infinite range of pluses and minuses each individual is born with, would mean, to begin with, a government of almost infinite scope and power.... And it would be just a completely screwed up mess for government even to attempt such a hopeless task of ensuring that an inherently unfair thing like life is somehow forced by government decree to become fair."

The fact that equality of opportunity was impossible to achieve did not render it a meaningless concept. It was a goal to be worked towards. In the end, everybody could not be made equal; nonetheless, society could strive to become more equal. Policies to spread opportunity more widely could have a positive impact, even when everybody knew that in the end, a perfect state of equality would never be reached.

Acceptance of the inherent inequalities in the world was not an excuse for the individual to give up. Rather, some respondents discussed a more pragmatic outlook on equality of opportunity that sought to use the opportunities and resources one did have to better one's life. They said, "I would agree somewhat.... Like we discussed earlier, you know, our government can only do so much....maybe a baseline, but in the end it's really up to the individual to accept -- to accept what they're given in life and try to take what they have and expand it. I'd be in the middle of the road on that."

What Societal Actions Are Necessary?

Respondents were asked what societal actions were necessary to make sure that everyone has an equal opportunity to succeed. Individuals differed substantially in their assessments of what actions were necessary. Some respondents believed that no new actions were necessary, and that the U.S. largely had achieved conditions of equal opportunity. He noted, "Now I don't think any actions are required. I think that we've more or less reached that point."

Some respondents viewed the problem of equal opportunity primarily as an issue that would need to be dealt with through the application and enforcement of laws against discrimination. There were limits to how much social change could be engineered. When discussing social actions that were necessary to ensure equal opportunity, one respondent said that the actions necessary were, "Mostly legal protection and active monitoring to make sure that those legal protections are being honored. And it's not perfect, but I think people are genuinely trying and I think that it will get better over time. I don't know that there's anything more you can do right now because it just takes -- society has to change as a whole. We still have people out there who are just incredible bigots or incredible this or that. We just have to wait for them to die off, for some of those opinions to change over time."

A wide variety of societal actions were mentioned, including accommodating the disabled, eliminating redlining in bank lending, housing programs, affirmative action, legal protections against discrimination, training programs, Title 9, improving public schools, employment programs and government subsidies. Education was the most common policy that respondents mentioned when discussing societal actions needed to ensure equal opportunity. Education was mentioned by 54 percent (15/28) of those interviewed.

Why Should Society Do What Is Necessary?

Respondents were also asked why society should take actions to ensure equal opportunity. Some respondents had a difficult time with this, since they believed this was self-evident. Individuals provided a range of reasons this should be so, including that it was the American way, that it was a moral obligation, that it ensured human dignity and that it produced a more efficient society. A number of individuals discussed how it was a necessary part of democratic social arrangements that required majority support for government. Other respondents argued that it was important to ensure equal opportunity because a lack of opportunity created social unrest and violence.

Equal opportunity was a universally accepted principle among those I talked to. It was a moral imperative, and it was good for business. It was a benefit that every good society should provide, and a foundation on which to build a good society. It was necessary to prevent social unrest. It was good for the economy and a component of human dignity.

Equal opportunity was an impossible ideal and many disagreed on its specific content and the policy implications that flowed from trying to attain it. For some it implied affirmative action, while others thought that affirmative action was a violation of the principle of equal opportunity. Some thought America already had achieved the basic conditions of equal opportunity, while others pointed out the vast disparities that characterized society. Differences in quality between public school systems were a common concern among many individuals.

While respondents had little doubt of the value of equal opportunity, they also balanced it against other values. Having no opportunity to interview respondents who were against "doing whatever is necessary to ensure equal opportunity" I can only speculate as to why individuals in the NES have historically been ambivalent with regard to this question. Some respondents I interviewed did express a belief that society could go too far in trying to obtain equal opportunity. Some ambivalence on this question may be generated by the feelings of some that there are limits to governmental and societal action, and the policies of the government are often blunt instruments.

The tendency of some respondents to qualify their response with the statement that "life isn't fair" also suggests that some were skeptical of the ability of society to achieve the conditions for equal opportunity. Many seemed willing to accept substantial inequalities as part of the human condition. This may also be another source for ambivalence with respect to this question.

We Have Gone Too Far in Pushing Equal Rights in This Country.

One of the questions used to measure beliefs about equality on the NES asks respondents to agree or disagree with the following statement: "We have gone too far in pushing equal rights in this country."

Of the respondents interviewed, only 14 percent (4/28) either agreed strongly or agreed with this statement. Individuals overwhelmingly rejected this statement, with 82 percent (23/28) either disagreeing or disagreeing strongly. There was relatively little direct expression of ambivalence, with only 7 percent (2/28) respondents expressing difficulty answering the question due to conflicted strong feelings. Approximately 46 percent (13/28) respondents did discuss considerations both for and against the statement when answering. There were no references to the President, the administration or political parties, indicating that there may not be much partisan framing associated with this question.

References to specific issues of the day were fairly common, and 68 percent of respondents (19/28) mentioned specific issues that might commonly be read about in a daily newspaper. Issues of the day were coded to include such issues as affirmative action or the glass ceiling. There was little confusion about what this statement meant, and only 4 percent (1/28) respondents directly expressed confusion.

Approximately 46 percent (13/28) respondents made a direct reference to African Americans. References to affirmative action were common, but were only mentioned by 36 percent (10/28) of those interviewed. Respondents mentioned a wide array of other groups, including Latinos, gays, the disabled, women, men, the old, veterans, religious people, illegal immigrants, and Jews. Respondents had a number of different interpretations of what pushing equal rights too far meant, and which groups this statement referred to. These are discussed in greater detail below.

Different Dimensions of Group Equality

Even when respondents made reference to race relations, they often interpreted the meaning of this question differently. For instance, some older respondents thought this question referred to segregation, while other respondents mentioned affirmative action. One respondent said, "What does that statement make me think of? It makes me think the person who made it and doesn't really want equal rights for other people." Another person framed the question in a historical context, noting that the statement "pushing equal rights too far" made them think of, "Segregation. Because I grew up during the time where you had the colored balcony, you had the colored water fountain, White water fountain.... Restaurants that said White only, and at the time they had separate, but equal, and they were separate, but they were not equal. They could not offer the same opportunities."

Reference to women's rights was almost as common as discussion of race. Approximately 39 percent (10/28) of respondents referred to women's rights when they discussed the statement. Individuals often talked of pay inequities between men and women, and the glass ceiling. Respondents who referred to women's rights often did not believe equal rights had been pushed too far because they saw current social conditions as being inherently unequal. ,

A number of respondents said that you can't push equal rights too far. By definition, equal rights were something that was good for everyone, and you can't have too much equality. One person argued, "Because I don't know if you can go too far, then you're not promoting equal rights anymore. If you've gone too far then somebody is going to be more equal than others. I don't think you can ever go too far in promoting equal rights because when you go too far then they're not equal rights anymore."

Inequalities Are Widespread

Many respondents pointed to existing inequalities in society as an indication that equal rights had not been pushed too far. When there were so many disparities between the treatment different genders, races, sexual orientations or ethnicities, it was hard for them to imagine that equal rights had been pushed too far. One man argued that it was not the case that equal rights had been pushed too far, "Because gay people can't get married. Because black people are systematically poorer. Because women still argue with people over a choice to get an abortion and women still make less money than men statistically. Mainly because we're not equal, so if we're not equal on as many levels as possible then we're obviously not doing enough."

For some, differences in economic opportunities were a greater source of disparity than discrimination against minorities. Equal rights had not been pushed too far because there were large differences in the resources available to different segments of society. Economic inequalities were corrosive to equal rights. Society had not done enough to remedy these inequalities. One respondent noted, "I think of the incredible disparity between minorities and people under the poverty level versus the rich families, you know….we have done an okay job of lessening racism and we have done an okay job of saying …okay, we're going to make sure that our college has a representation of all these different minority groups, but we haven't done a good job of making sure that everybody when it gets to the point where they're applying for the job or when they get to the point that they're in college that they have the same, the same background and resources to call on."

Pushing equal rights meant different things to different respondents. For some, it meant obtaining basic rights, such as the right to vote, or the right to be free from legal discrimination. For others, equal rights implied greater access to wealth or other social resources that would enable one to compete on a level playing field.

Conflicts with Other Values: Why Only Somewhat?

Some respondents did qualify their response in certain ways, indicating that their endorsement for equality was limited by other values that were also important. One respondent, who somewhat disagreed that equality had been pushed too far, argued that there might be cases where pushing equal rights could create too much government interference into private decision making. While he stressed the importance of equality, he also noted, "It's just a real risk if you have too many bureaucrats monitoring everything…what we do in terms of hiring, promotions and all these kinds of things."

Some respondents who agreed with the statement were ambivalent. They were torn between believing in equal rights, and what they saw as the negative repercussions of affirmative action or other policies that were being used to push equal rights. In the same breath, these respondents could both endorse and reject policies to advance equal rights. They endorsed the basic values and goals of the program, but they rejected the specific execution. When asked what pushing equal rights made them think of, one noted, "Well, I think of affirmative action and stuff like that, which is a really good idea and I think it was a good idea at the time, but just you're going to give it to somebody based on like race or gender that is like -- what if they're a horrible employee? …you should have the best man for the job. It should be merit based."

Some respondents made a distinction between groups that were legitimately disadvantaged, and others that were not. Pushing equal rights had not gone far enough in the African American community. The proliferation of disadvantaged groups demanding "equal rights" did have a limit. One African American man noted, "There's still problems with various minority groups that are not making headway even with the benefits that are being provided. African Americans, there's still a high proportion that are -- that don't have the opportunities that others have. I don't want to get involved in the whole, you know, everybody is a minority kind of thing and everybody ought to have a protected class, be a member of a protected class. I think that goes a little bit too far….but there are major sections of our country which still suffer even after 40 years discrimination and if it wasn't there we would revert back to the old ways. Go down to Mississippi. If you took equal opportunity laws out of existence they'd be back to Jim Crow in two minutes, you know. So I think it needs to continue."

To a great extent, beliefs about pushing equal rights are tied to the specific group that one applies them too. While membership in a minority group tends to make one disagree that equal rights have been pushed too far, a number of individuals qualified their answer, depending on the specific group considered. Competition among minority groups can make some minority respondents question the rights claims of other groups. This was the source of some ambivalence for some minority respondents.

We Have Gone Too Far

While most respondents disagreed with the statement that we had gone too far pushing equal rights, a number of people did agree with this statement. In some cases, individuals who very strongly endorsed the value of equality also thought that it was possible to go too far. For them, pushing equal rights too far meant employing policies that were too heavy handed, contentious and ultimately not effective. One noted, "In some ways I do agree with that statement. I know that sounds contradictory, but I do think in some ways it's overemphasized. You know, I believe in equal opportunity, I believe in government playing a part in that, but I also see where it can kind of be overdone to the point where reverse discrimination happens ... either because in trying to provide equal opportunity I think some ways are better than others. ...You can tip the scales too much, not often, but it does happen in some cases. I just want to find a balance, for things to be true and equal I guess for all people."

Some argued that pushing equal opportunity too far meant reverse discrimination. With so much attention being paid to safeguarding minority rights, the concerns of the majority were not taken into consideration. One respondent said, "I think they have a double standard. They say that they are going to be behind equal rights yet they give more floor space to the outspoken people, whatever that group may be."

One woman answered this question by referring to religious freedom. She argued that concern for the minority who was offended by the display of religious sentiments ultimately led to a loss of rights for the majority. Another woman argued that pushing equal rights too far meant making unreasonable claims for equal treatment. There were natural inequalities between individuals and sometimes between men and women. In competition for physically demanding jobs, women would tend to be at a disadvantage. Legal protections against discrimination should be balanced against the need for employers to hire people who could best do the job.

Black Ambivalence toward Equality

One African American respondent did endorse the belief that we had gone too far in pushing equal rights. In his case, it was the success of immigrants that led him to speculate that immigrants were the recipient of special treatment. He noted, "And I'm saying some people have more rights than others, especially non-Americans. To me they've got more rights than others and they're here and they got more rights than us. And we call it equal opportunity? No, they're making it better for them and you're not doing to me, you're not doing right for your own citizens that were born here, my birthright …Like I say, I'm not knocking nobody coming over here. But what about poor Joe Blow? He want to do the same thing, but he don't have the opportunities, he don't know where to go to start. If you take somebody from another country and lead them by the hand and put it right on there, then that person there he thinks he's better than you, you know, because now he feel that you were lazy, you had nothing to do."

While this question did reflect beliefs about inter-group rivalry, it was not always the case that it tapped into the social and economic insecurity of the majority over gains and advancement of minorities. It also tapped into the fears that some minority groups might be favored at the expense of other minority groups.

Affirmative Action

Respondents referred to affirmative action in about a third of the responses. For a number of respondents, pushing equal rights too far meant using racial preferences to promote equality. One retired man argued, "Because I think we have simply adopted a mindless, moronic policy of reverse discrimination.... Whatever was wrong about the pre-civil rights race relations is now simply to be inverted a hundred and eighty degrees. And that somehow makes it right....The theory is not discrimination against Blacks is wrong...discrimination in favor of Blacks is now right...Whereas, my view would be discrimination period, discrimination of any sort on the basis of things like race and sex and so forth is wrong."

Personal experiences with affirmative action often led respondents to agree that society had gone too far in pushing equal rights. One woman was skeptical of office diversity policy. She noted, "Because I've seen too many incompetent people working and maybe it was to -- maybe they were hired because they needed to hire a black person, they needed to hire a Hispanic, and so they kind of evened it out, you know....I think it should be based on competence and not on representing a certain group....you know, having the whole rainbow in your office. Do you know what I mean?"

Individuals were often either ambivalent or virulently opposed to affirmative action. Conflicts between equality before the law, equality of opportunity and equality of outcome were most prevalent when considering affirmative action.

Respondents discussed a range of issues and minority groups when they answered this question. While references to women and African Americans were the most common, individuals also mentioned a wide array of other minority or disadvantaged classes of people. Some thought this question referred to segregation, while others discussed affirmative action or other policies associated with discrimination. Some ambivalence in the response to this question was associated with conflicts between different dimensions of equality. It may be the case that those who believe most fervently in equality are likely to be ambivalent if they believe this question refers to affirmative action.

Positive responses to the question appear to be associated not only with majority-minority conflicts, but also with intergroup rivalries between minority groups. As such, some ambivalence toward this question may also be generated by conflicts between one's minority status, and feelings towards other minority groups. For instance, if being African American may tend to pre-dispose you towards believing that equal rights haven't been pushed too far, negative assessments of other minority groups may tend to make one answer that equal rights for those groups have been pushed too far.

Since individuals referred to such a wide array of groups whose rights should be considered, a significant amount of ambivalence may be associated with whether one considers oneself to be part of the majority, or the minority pushing for equal rights. For instance, while one might assume that a white male is part of the majority, individuals referred to the rights of fathers, veterans, the disabled, the old, the poor and Jews. One's frame of reference as to what minority rights are being considered, and what groups are relevant to answering the question could change how one answers.

One of the Big Problems in this Country is that We Don't Give Everyone an Equal Chance.

Another one of the questions that measures equality asks individuals to respond to the following statement: "One of the big problems in this country is that we don't give everyone an equal chance". Respondents could agree, agree strongly, neither agree nor disagree, disagree or disagree strongly. The interviewees were more divided about how to answer this question. Half of the respondents (14/28) either agreed or strongly agreed. Approximately 14 percent (4/28) neither agreed nor disagreed, while the remaining 36 percent (10/28) expressed some level of disagreement. Respondents were often torn about how to answer this question because they typically endorsed both the value of social equality and also the personal responsibility of the individual. For some, admitting that everyone didn't have an equal chance implied that individuals lacked the power to improve themselves. Most respondents did not want to believe that individuals were powerless to make themselves better. Some of this was expressed directly as ambivalence, with 25 percent (7/28) of respondents expressing conflicted feelings about reconciling their beliefs about equality and individualism. It was also common for people to express considerations both for and against their position when responding, and 43 percent (12/28) of the interviewees did this.

Individuals did not overtly express partisanship when they answered this question. None of them referred to the President, the Administration or political parties. Only one respondent expressed confusion over what the question was asking.

Approximately 43 percent (12/28) of individuals referred to "issues of the day" when responding. Issues of the day were interpreted to be specific issues that one might read about in the daily paper. Respondents referred to a broad range of issues, including funding for education, the high percentage of black males in prison, training programs and the riots in Paris among others.

Respondents did not interpret this question to be about any particular type of inequality. Only 18 percent (5/28) specifically mentioned African Americans when they

responded, and there were no mentions of women. Another
14 percent referred specifically to wealth, and a number of
other respondents discussed economic inequalities more
generally.   Individuals often referred to discrimination in a
generic sense without referencing a specific group.
Respondents thus had a number of different interpretations of
this question. While some focused on discrimination, others
tended to discuss inequalities associated with economic
disparities.

Many respondents discussed discrimination generally,
or referred to specific groups that were discriminated against.
Respondents tended to differ in their beliefs on how
widespread discrimination was and what its sources were.
While some believed discrimination was rampant, others
believed that it was caused by a bigoted minority.

Support for Macro-Equality

A number of respondents discussed an equal chance in a
broader economic context. One individual argued that
everybody did not have an equal chance because, "…you have
children being born into very poor families. Economically
they don't have the same opportunities as children born into
wealthy families…." Some discussed a more expansive set of
social resources, including parental educational attainment,
family structure, wealth and a safe social environment. One
needed to consider the full spectrum of resources that were
available to the individual. No one could truly argue that
everybody had an equal chance when there were such vast
differences in what was available to different levels of society.

Reconciling Limited Government and the Need to Provide Equal Chances

A number of individuals seemed to struggle with how to reconcile their beliefs about equality of opportunity with other values. For instance, individuals balanced the need to provide an equal chance with the increases in spending and government programs that might be required to achieve it.

Another respondent rejected the basic premise of the question. Assuming that there was a "we" that could provide everybody with an equal chance was a mistake. It wasn't within the power of government to provide this to people. He noted,

"Because I don't think it is -- the phrasing we don't give everyone an equal chance means that there is some we out there, probably the government, whose job it is to look over everyone's shoulder and make sure everyone does have an equal chance. And there is no we that can achieve such a program, at least not until you can ensure that every child is born with the same IQ and the same health potential and on and on…So, to imagine there is any sort of a "we" that could ensure people are given an equal chance is a -- I think a completely erroneous pre-text."

Conflicts between Equal Chances and Equal Outcomes

Individuals were asked what they thought an equal chance meant. In general, an equal chance was defined as being a lack of discrimination and a merit based system were individuals competed based on their talents and abilities. One man said that an equal chance was,

"Taking the person just as a person, giving that person, without any prejudgments an opportunity to prove who they are, and do that the same to next person, and the next person, regardless of their race, what they look like, what they sound like, who they are, where they come from, giving each and every person the same non-prejudging opportunity"

Respondents were torn between recognizing that inequalities would be created by competition between individuals, and the desire to remedy historical inequities. It was clear that ambivalence for some was caused by the tension between their belief in meritocracy and their simultaneous desire to have more equality in society. In the same breath, an individual could proclaim the desirability of meritocracy and also expound on the need for programs to provide the disadvantaged with a little extra help. One person noted that an equal chance, "Just means that -- given the same situation you perform according to your skills, that you are able to perform according to -- yeah. But then I also believe on some level if the reason why you're behind to begin with is because of some historical inequity, I do believe that you should also be helped a little as well."

For some respondents, distinguishing between legal equality and equality of resources allowed them to resolve the conflict between their belief in equality and their endorsement of a system of competition that produced inequality. One person argue that an equal chance was,

"Equal access to, you know, our society in every sort of function of its existence -- education, housing, work. Those are the principal ones. An opportunity to -- as any other citizen of this nation, an opportunity available to the richest man. But that doesn't mean that there's an equality in terms of wealth, but there is an equal opportunity to the protection by the legal system."

Ambivalence – Social versus Individual Explanations

Overall, this question generated a great deal of

ambivalence. At the heart of this ambivalence was the desire of individuals to recognize that there were significant inequalities in the world, while at the same time believing that the future of an individual was not determined by their surroundings. Obviously there were enormous differences in the resources in terms of education, wealth and status. Very few would argue that these resources were irrelevant to the final outcome. At the same time, most everybody believed that individuals still could determine their own fate. One person noted the following,

"No, I'm kind of in the middle on this one. I think -- I think that people -- people are always going to be -- there's always going to be unfortunate circumstances out there, but there's plenty of people in there who have risen up from destitute, Horatio Alger type stories, who have risen up from poor conditions to make it….So I think that's what makes living in America so much better than anywhere else. But there is a lot of people who -- people who -- their schools are horrible, you know. There's crime and poverty all around them, so it's a lot harder. But -- so I'm kind of in the middle of the road because if you want it bad enough anybody can get it."

One respondent who was an independent construction contractor who frequently worked with recent immigrants noted, "You know, a work ethic, a different work ethic, will bring more opportunity even if you're a minority group. But again, you know, there are always parts of society that are going to be left behind and equal opportunity is meant to address that."

Across many responses, individuals stressed both the importance of individual behavior for taking advantage of opportunities, while at the same time recognizing and wanting to remedy systemic resource inequalities. Even when respondents argued for social programs, they also insisted that they be based on and incorporate elements of individualism. One woman argued, "Well, I think we could do more for our less fortunate people, but then again it's up to them to take advantage of those kind of -- you know, you can put out your hand but it doesn't mean they're going to take it."

These results are consistent with numerous other public opinion studies that show that Americans tend to endorse social programs such as training or jobs programs that emphasize individualistic solutions over redistributive programs that are based on systemic explanations of poverty (Kluegel and Smith 1986).

The Land of Opportunity

Many respondents related the idea of an equal chance to the idea of America as the land of opportunity. A number of them compared the opportunities available in America to other parts of the world. One person noted, "We have a fine country here that does give people -- anybody a chance. If they are willing to go out there and get it…." In some cases, respondents seemed to acknowledge a certain level of ambivalence about America being the land of opportunity. They were attached to this ideal, but they often recognized that it didn't capture the complete story. Another said, "Everybody does have an equal chance, that you can make your opportunities, that you can overcome adversity…At the same time sometimes it's very difficult to find access to those opportunities." Respondents seemed to want individuals to acknowledge and take advantage of the opportunities available, while at the same time, not to blind themselves to the problems of American society.

Overall, individuals displayed a relatively high level of ambivalence in answering this question. Respondents were attached to the idea of an equal chance and the U.S. as a land of opportunity. The belief that one was in control of one's own destiny and that one only needed to act to improve one's fortunes was a powerful belief among most. Many also simultaneously endorsed the need to improve the prospects of some members of society due to inequities.

If People Were Treated More Equally in this Country We Would Have Many Fewer Problems.

Another question on equality asked respondents to agree or disagree with the following statement: "If people were treated more equally in this country we would have many fewer problems." Of those I talked to, 54 percent (15/28) either agreed somewhat or agreed strongly with the statement. A significant number, approximately 21 percent (6/28) neither agreed nor disagreed with the statement. The remaining 25 percent did not agree. Direct expressions of ambivalence were not that common, with only 11 percent (3/28) respondents saying that it was difficult to answer the question because of conflicted strong feelings. Levels of ambivalence may have been lowered somewhat by the relatively high percentage answering in the middle, as noted above. Many of the respondents did discuss considerations both for and against the statement while answering, with 50 percent doing this. This is notable since the follow up questions did not specifically probe for arguments for and against the statement.

Partisan framing of this question was not detected. None of the interviewees referred to the President, the administration or political parties. Confusion about the meaning of the question was limited. Only 7 percent (2/28) respondents directly expressed confusion over how to interpret the question. It was common for individuals to discuss their answer by referring to issues of the day. Issues of the day included subjects such as education, crime, the riots in Paris, housing, credit ratings, the drug epidemic, tolerance of gays, and hurricane Katrina. Individuals interpreted the question in a variety of different ways. Inequality was often interpreted within the context of racial, gender or other group based discrimination. Of those answering, 75 percent referred to discrimination. Many respondents referred to economic inequality when answering as well, with 50 percent mentioning class based differences between the poor and the rest of society. References to crime were also very common. When asked to discuss problems that would be alleviated by greater equality, 43 percent of respondents (12/28) discussed crime.

Respondents frequently discussed discrimination. Some respondents discussed specific groups. For instance, 29 percent (8/28) discussed African Americans, 46 percent referred to a specific race or the category of race, 7 percent (2/28) referred to gays, 11 percent (3/28) referred to gender and 21 percent (6/28) mentioned the poor. A significant fraction of respondents, 36 percent (10/28), referred to no specific groups when they answered.

Natural Inequalities

While racial groups tended to dominate the discussion, interviewees mentioned a variety of other groups that were treated unequally, including the old, short people, ugly people and immigrants. Respondents beliefs about equal treatment sometimes depended on the groups they discussed. Thus for instance, some respondents who were skeptical that equal treatment could help solve society's problems chose to discuss intractable inequalities between groups that are not typically characterized as being discriminated against. There is no doubt that society discriminates in favor of beautiful people or tall people. Income is correlated with height, even though height is important to actual job performance in only a small number of professions. Nonetheless, most people view these types of inequalities as part of a set of natural inequalities and unfair practices that are not damaging to society.

One's assessment of equality depends to a great extent on whether one considers the value in the abstract, or in reference to a particular group. If one considers the question within the context of a particular group, which group one thinks about and one's feelings about that group play an important role in shaping belief. The frame of reference as to what groups are relevant when considering the value of equality has a great impact on how one answers this question. Some instability over time in how respondents answer this question may be caused by changes in the group frame that respondents consider when they answer.

Problems Caused by Inequality

Respondents differed on what problems they thought could be remedied by reducing inequalities. Reducing inequalities referred both to addressing the effects of race and poverty. One person simply said, "Well, if we never had slaves, we would have fewer problems." Inequalities were dangerous because people that were socially isolated with no prospects for advancement were dangerous. One person noted, "I think people who are not treated equally have a higher propensity for anger, and they act out on that anger..."

The failure of society to provide upward mobility to all groups created pockets of poverty that were the sources of serious social problems. Respondents considered a range of groups when they discussed this danger, including urban and rural poverty, immigrants and racial groups. One person noted, "In this area we have transients that pick apples and other things. And, of course, they bring their families with them. If, as a county, we provide education for those children, so that not isolating them into one pattern, so that they can

never get out of picking crops. And the same way in the
slums. That there ought to be good schools available for them
to go to. And the slum condition, whatever is causing the
slum, needs to be improved."

As noted above, 43 percent (12/28) of respondents
discussed crime as a problem that was caused by inequality.
Respondents who thought that inequality caused crime had
somewhat different interpretations of how they were related.
For some, inequalities caused crime because minorities were
often demonized and preyed on by the majority. Reducing
inequalities would limit racial tension and race based crimes.
One person noted, "Well, I think some problems …that would
mean things like hate crimes, and riots, and that kind of
thing."

For others, inequality caused crime because individuals
with few prospects would find criminal activity a more
attractive prospect. One argued, "If people were treated more
equally, it would help with employment issues, it would help
spread the monetary wealth, redistribute it more fairly, so that
there would be less crime…" Inequalities created individuals
and groups that had no stake in society and no particular
reason to play by the rules. Another person noted, "Where
you don't give opportunity you breed people that are going to
take their opportunity I'd say by force, one way or another."

Conflicts with Limited Government

For some, lawsuits and public organizations tasked with
promoting equal rights were the problems that needed to be
solved. One person noted, "Ok, and the statement is, if people
were treated more equally, they would have fewer problems,
what would the fewer problems be? Well, we wouldn't have
the equal employment opportunity commission. We wouldn't
have the EEOC. I don't know, that's all I can think of offhand.
There wouldn't be a lot of agencies, arbitrators or mediators

involved, because we wouldn't have those problems anymore, we wouldn't have huge lawsuit settlements because so and so was overlooked at the job at Wal-Mart, so we're going to settle for $741 million dollars, I mean, come on, we wouldn't have these huge lawsuits that tie up the courts."

While initially I found the above interpretation of the problems of inequality to be rather quirky, it was mentioned by enough people that I wondered about its significance. For some, the social programs and laws set up to remedy discrimination in our society have themselves become the problem. This interpretation of the question was shared by respondents who described themselves as liberal as well as a least one respondent who was African American.

While some might see government as an instrument to promote equality, another respondent speculated that government policies might actually lead to less equality. He noted, "What I think of is what I see on a lot of different levels. I see some minorities still kept in situations where there is poverty, where there is lower economics, they're not given the opportunity, sometimes I feel it is almost planned, this is the way the big picture is, and I wonder who planned that, could it be big government? You know?"

While fairly liberal, this respondent was also often skeptical of the effectiveness of government programs. His ideals for government action were often frustrated by his experience with bureaucracy. This suspicion permeated many of his answers.

Conflicts between Different Dimensions of Equality

A woman who disagreed took issue with the specific methods used to treat people more equally. For her, the statement implied race preferences and unequal treatment. Seeing society as mostly diverse and achieving a high level of racial balance, she did not like these policies. She noted, "Because I think the United States, it seems to embrace all this diversity. So that's why I don't agree. I mean, for example, look at the Supreme Court. Everybody was so happy when we had a woman on the Supreme Court. Then we got a Jew, and then we got a black, and now they're pushing a Hispanic. Why do we have to judge them on that stuff? Why? It doesn't make any sense. Maybe we'll get an Asian-American and maybe we'll get an Indian-American….And for me it's at the point of absurdity. Vote for the competent judge period, you know what I mean? Who cares about where he's from, who cares what group is representative. It's just that – it's just gone way too far."

There was some uncertainty over what social domains this question applied to. While some respondents argued that legal equality had already largely been achieved in the U.S., they were ambivalent when they discussed the need to reduce other economic and social inequalities. Their response to the question varied according to whether they discussed legal equality or economic equality.

Some Problems Are Intractable

One respondent, who considered the statement primarily in a material context, argued that the problem of economic inequality was intractable. Inherent and natural inequalities would always be translated into economic differences in wealth. The basic premise of the question, that these inequalities could be remedied, was flawed. He said, "Because I think a lot of the problems in America can't be – aren't going to be eliminated by people treating each other more fairly or having more equal protection….Because they're just problems that every society has that are just -- that have been with the world since the beginning of time. There will always be poor people, there will always be, you know, old people. No matter what you do some people won't have access to things or they'll be too stupid to take advantage of it. So in terms of economic problems I don't think necessarily that treating people more equally will solve a lot of our economic problems."

The problem of inequality was intractable for others because it could not be reached through legislation. Some types of discrimination could not be addressed through the law, and would never be eliminated. For him, "How do I think people could be treated more equally? Well, I think a lot of times -- I think the existing laws for the most part should be enforced. That's probably the best way. Some things just can't be legislated. I can't -- you know, good looking people are always going to have an advantage and there's no law that can be passed that will ever eliminate that….or tall people are always going to be afforded certain -- are going to be treated differently than short and there's nothing I can – there's nothing I can do about that…"

The frame of reference of the respondent was often critical to how they answered the question. When viewed abstractly, respondents often discussed the impossibility of obtaining equality. If viewed from the perspective of specific social and economic problems, many interviewees argued for the necessity of improving current conditions.

Conflicts between Equality of Opportunity and Equality of Outcome

Respondents often sought to justify existing inequalities. For them, inequalities were natural. One argued, "I am afraid I would have to say neither agree nor disagree…Because there -- there would be no good in treating people more equally, as long as people are unequal.-- To simply pretend they are not, I don't think would give us fewer problems. I think it would give us more problems."

The vision of a society that was totally equal was seen as implausible, and maybe even a bit boring. A number of respondents defended current social conditions, arguing that equal opportunities were provided to the extent that it was possible. To seek greater equality was to try to move towards an artificially contrived egalitarian society. One respondent argued both that society could not be made more equal, and that it would be wrong to make society more equal even if it could be. They seemed to reject both the feasibility and the moral underpinnings of egalitarianism.

They noted, "Well, that is hard. I know you are going to see a lot of poor people that are going to say yes, if I had what you had or -- if I had what they had, it would be better….But do we owe everybody if you don't get out doing work? I don't think so….I am middle line on this …if everybody had the same income all across the United States and everybody, you know, had the same house and the same cars and -- what could anybody holler about. You know? But can you really be in a society like that? I mean I still believe the opportunity is there. I realize when you are poor or you don't have education, you may think that it is not there. Maybe you can't get the opportunity. I disagree. I think the opportunities are there."

The statement that society would have many fewer problems if people were treated more equally implies that equality has social utility. Some individuals argued against this on two separate fronts. They saw a utility in inequality, but they also justified inequality in moral terms as well. They thought that individuals should not only seek to obtain material equality, but also to work to deserve such rewards in a moral sense.

While respondents didn't tend to openly express ambivalence when they answered this question, their responses did highlight a number of factors that could cause instability in response over time to this question.

When respondents discussed discrimination they

sometimes discussed the concept in the abstract and sometimes referred to specific groups. Respondents had differing feelings about particular groups, and their group frame of reference likely had an important impact on how they answered.

It was clear that a number of respondents considered this question within the context of other values as well. Some respondents mentioned the size and limits of government power as a consideration that was relevant when considering whether society's problems could be remedied by treating people more equally. At least some respondents who cherished equality were concerned that it could conflict with other deeply held beliefs. The domain in which equality was considered (social, political, economic) was also relevant to an individual's response. Changes in the domain frame that was used to answer this question caused responses to differ with respect to this question.

It Is Not Really that Big a Problem If Some People Have More of a Chance in Life than Others.

Another question on equality asked respondents to agree or disagree with the following statement. "It is not really that big a problem if some people have more of a chance in life than others."

More than half of those interviewed disagreed with this question. Approximately 63 percent (17/28) of those interviewed either disagreed, or strongly disagreed. Most respondents did not directly express ambivalence. About 15 percent (4/28) respondents had a difficult time answering because of conflicting strong feelings. It appeared that ambivalence about this question ran much deeper than this relatively low percentage would indicate. Approximately 56 percent (15/28) of respondents discussed considerations both for and against the statement. In fact, even respondents who selected an answer to the question fairly easily, and thus were not classified as being ambivalent, often later indicated in their extended answer that they really simultaneously held beliefs that would allow them to answer in either direction.

Partisanship did not appear to play a large role in response to this question. Only 4 percent (1/28) of respondents mentioned the President, the administration or political parties when they answered. Only one person expressed confusion over what the question meant. Respondents seemed to interpret this question to be primarily about inequalities of wealth. About 85 percent (23/28) respondents mentioned economic inequalities, while only 7 percent (2/28) mentioned discrimination.

Overall, answers to this question were often qualified by a variety of considerations, conflicting beliefs and interpretations of the question. While most respondents considered this question to be primarily about inequalities of wealth, education and status, their answer was often different depending on the frame of reference that they used to consider the question. It depended whether respondents considered inequality within the context of society or on an individual basis. They often argued for the existence of opportunities for everybody and the ability of everybody to make it, while at the same time disliking the overall levels of equality in society. It also mattered whether they considered inequalities within the context of those who were wealthy, or thought about the bottom rungs of the economic ladder. Individuals were less concerned about capping extreme wealth, than they were about ensuring that there was a floor beneath which no one should fall. While many viewed inequalities as unfair, they also often argued that inequality was inevitable.

There was a surprising consistency in how individuals discussed what the statement meant. Most respondents believed that "some people have more of a chance" referred primarily to economic disparities related to family wealth. Family money, high priced education and personal connections were the primary types of advantages that respondents discussed. One person noted, "What does it make me think of -- maybe a community college versus Yale or Harvard. You know? Some people can't go to Yale or Harvard. But, I mean -- but there are other ways to get educated." Other types of disparities, such as health, good role models and a strong family environment were also mentioned by some.

Even though respondents often expressed dislike for the inequality, they would often qualify their statement by noting that there were other ways for individuals to get ahead. Remarkably, some of the strongest advocates of equality had less strong feelings about inequalities related to wealth. They may not have liked these inequalities, but they had a difficult time denouncing them either.

Another source of inequality was the personal networks and favoritism that children of successful parents had access to. The inequalities related to being born into wealthy and successfully families were unfair, but many respondents thought that it was impossible for society to prevent this type of favoritism. Some ambivalence with regard to this question was caused by the tension between what was fair in the abstract, and the belief that it was natural for parents to try to provide advantages for their children. The individual impulse of parents to help their progeny was positive, but the overall collective social impacts were often unfair and not representative of their belief in meritocracy.

Individualism

Beliefs about equality were qualified by the individualistic beliefs of some respondents. It was more important for individuals to focus on what they could control, rather than worrying about what they did not have. For many, if you worked hard enough, you could make you own opportunities. One person noted, "I would disagree. It wouldn't necessarily be a problem….You get out of life what you put in. You can't constantly worry about what someone else is doing. You have got to take care of yourself, and everything else just falls into place"

Some believed that having to work hard and struggle ultimately made individuals stronger. One person noted, "Well, I don't expect everything to be equal. Sometimes it builds character when you deal with challenges."

Many respondents struggled to rectify their belief in the power of the individual to overcome their circumstances with their belief that more equality was desirable. One individual noted that "our problems aren't going to go away if we give people equal footing. It's really what they do with it. So it is a big deal if we're not arming everybody with the same amount of information or similar opportunities…." Providing some level of opportunity for all was more important than providing total equality.

Personal experiences shaped the beliefs of some. Those who had overcome obstacles to achieve success believed in the system. Having been able to climb the economic ladder, they were less likely to argue that social inequalities provided immovable barriers to personal advancement and success. One woman noted the following, "I think that's true that some people have more of a chance, but I do think they can -- that it can even out if you look for it. I mean, I'm a great example because I grew up on welfare in tenement housing in Iowa. And my mother worked in factories, she worked in -- she worked as a cleaning lady, jobs like that. And we didn't have money for college and I got financial aid, I got grants, I went to college. I've done a lot of things and I could have grown up and become just like my mom but I didn't, and the fact that I'm not -- I wasn't privileged, there are a few privileged few, but the opportunities were there for me and so I was able to, you know, get an education, a degree and all that. There's always going to be a few, privileged few, but there are always opportunities for the unprivileged to move up."

Overall, respondents tended to be more ambivalent about economic inequalities. When considering society as a whole, individuals were troubled by disparities of wealth and resources. At the personal level, they found it natural that people should strive to make a better life for themselves and their family. When individuals exploited the opportunities available to them, inequalities were the natural result. The value of equality of opportunity thus conflicted with an abstract desire of many for a more equal overall distribution of wealth. Significant ambivalence arose among respondents when they tried to square their individualistic beliefs in equal opportunity with other dimensions of equality that were also important.

Discussion

Throughout these interviews, most respondents endorsed the value of equality strongly. At the same time, they were also often ambivalent when they considered equality because they perceived different types of equality and the conflicts between them. These results confirm the findings of many scholars (Feldman 2003; Feldman and Zaller 1992; Lane 1986; Kluegel and Smith 1986). There is a fundamental schism in public opinion. The value of equality when it is applied to the individual is associated with equal opportunity. When equality is considered in a social frame, as it applies to all of society, it tends to be associated with equality of outcome. Within this context, the value of equality of opportunity often conflicts with the value of equality of outcome. Equality is a multidimensional concept and the questions used to measure equality may not adequately distinguish between these different dimensions. Conflict within the value of equality itself is a source of significant ambivalence among the public.

These findings also indicate that ambivalence is widespread. In contrast to some scholars who have argued that ambivalence only exists for a few hard issues (Alvarez and Brehm 2002), these findings indicate that Americans are conflicted about the idea of equality itself, and the many specific issues it affects. There is significant ambivalence on such issues as economic redistribution, affirmative action and other issues where the value of equality of opportunity may conflict with equality of outcome.

Previous research has found that individuals generally support equality in the political and social domains of their life, but they are not egalitarians when it comes to the economic system (Hochschild 1981). An individual's selection of which domain the question referred to often seemed to determine their answer. Some respondents who were strong supporters of legal equality did not support equality within the context of the economy. These results confirm these findings. There is little ambivalence about social or political equality. The domain frame of reference in which the value of equality is considered may determine whether an individual is ambivalent about equality. The public is more ambivalent about economic equality, where conflicts between the different dimensions of equality are most apparent.

Previous research has suggested that less informed voters often make up their mind about specific policies to promote equality, not based on general principles, but rather based on their feelings for particular groups (Sniderman, Brody and Tetlock 1991; Hochschild 2006). Racial affect and an individual's group frame of reference can change how one expresses the value of equality. These results showed support for this thesis as well. Some respondents appeared to apply the value of equality differently based on which group was being considered.

These interview findings also support the thesis that people are attached to a belief in equal opportunity because it is linked to the individualistic idea that one does or should have control over one's fate. Those who were less fortunate often were the most individualistic and strongly attached to the idea that one must take responsibility for one's life. Equal opportunity and meritocratic achievement provided a way to make this possible. There was a strong attachment to the idea that America was a land of opportunity for most, and this served to mold how individuals thought about equality.

Individuals did not tend to discuss the value of equality within the framework of partisanship. These findings are at odds with those of McCann (1997), who has argued that partisanship can serve to shape belief in the value of equality.

Overall, the most important and widespread source of ambivalence among respondents was caused by the perceived conflict between the individualistic value of equal opportunity and the social value of equality of outcome. The dominant value dimension was equality of opportunity, but many respondents were deeply conflicted in their feelings about equality.

Conclusions about Equality

Values are substantive concepts. Much of the public does have meaningful values with respect to equality and these values affect how they think about specific political issues. At the same time, equality is a complex and multidimensional value. Equality harbors within itself a paradox that makes it difficult to apply for many. Equality before the law, equal opportunity and equality of outcome conflict with one another, although these are often all considered to represent a single dimension of equality.

Because of this, value framing matters for political persuasion. The group frame (gender, race, ethnicity, religion), the domain category (political, social, economic) and the personal frame (social versus individualistic) often influence what an individual will believe about equality. Between these different frames of equality, an individual can simultaneously believe different things about equality, and many in the public do.

Politicians who seek to convince the public of a course of action need to appeal to the value of equality, but this requires attention to the way equality is conceptualized within different frames of reference. There is significant room to promote libertarian solutions to public policy challenges. The public is individualistic, even in its belief in the value of equality. At the same time, the public also cares deeply about equality of outcome. Policies that seek to mitigate overall social inequalities within a policy framework that is individualistic and promotes personal responsibility will resonate best with the public. Policies that address social inequality at the expense of equal opportunity, meritocracy and the individual are on shaky ideological ground. The public may be of two minds on these programs.

Chapter 5: Conclusions

The findings of this research challenge the values paradigm in public opinion research and also suggest that the values of the modern public are significantly different than those described in historic studies of American culture. Values have typically been conceptualized by scholars as overarching beliefs that can affect numerous, more specific attitudes. Public opinion researchers working in the values paradigm have argued that values are different than attitudes because they are more stable over time and can be prioritized into value systems. Further, some scholars have made the case that values provide a means for citizens, who have little political knowledge and a limited conception of ideology, to organize their political thoughts and beliefs into a coherent structure.

Other research has shown that even individuals with stable values can exhibit significant instability in their attitudes because they may experience value conflicts or do not have sufficient information to connect their values to their attitudes. Nonetheless, many scholars start with the assumption that although attitudes may be unstable, values are conceptually different, of greater substance and more stable than attitudes.

While the concept of public opinion being organized around two or three overarching values may be appealing, in-depth interviews have shown individuals to be conflicted and ambivalent when given the opportunity to discuss their values in an open ended format. Individuals hold opposing ideas in their head and have difficulty prioritizing their values. The public's thinking about core values is often compartmentalized and individuals apply different values in different domains of life. Many individuals comfortably live with contradictory values and beliefs, even concerning the most basic values of equality and freedom. The findings of this research provide evidence for some of the sources of this ambivalence.

This research suggests that modern American values are substantively different than those portrayed in historical studies of American culture. Many scholars have argued that American political culture is defined by several core values. Historically these values have formed a value complex whose elements reinforced each other. For instance, equality before the law served as an important limitation of government. When the law applies equally to everyone, it was thought to serve as a check on the abuse of government authority by those in power. Similarly, a belief in natural God given rights was also seen to serve as a limitation on government. When rights were conceived to have a divine origin independent of government power, belief in transcendent and unchanging moral truths was thought to be consistent with the idea of limited government.

In early American history, limitation of government and economic individualism were seen as consistent with the value of equal opportunity. When economic rewards were determined in a market economy instead of by a mercantilist state, opportunities were spread more equally across society. Lastly, a robust civil society was thought to require, and be related to, limited government. Excessive centralization of resources and power in society were thought to enervate free, independent and voluntary action by the agents of civil society.

There is no definitive public opinion data with which to verify the above assertions about the historical value systems of early America, but many scholars have argued for this linkage of American political values. The results of this study stand opposed to this traditional conception of values. The public is ambivalent and conflicted about their core values.

This research described in this book was mostly drawn from in-depth interviews and some quantitative analysis of survey data. The purpose of the in-depth (or cognitive)

interviews was to obtain information on how respondents
think about the questions as they answer them. Cognitive
interviews help to identify interpretations of the question and
sources of error that may create ambivalence or instabilities in
the response. Quantitative analysis of NES data was used to
develop these findings further with a larger representative
sample of the entire U.S. population. A variety of statistical
techniques were employed on this larger sample, including
descriptive statistics and correlation analysis. This research
was also further developed with other statistical models such
as structural equation modeling and logistic regression
analysis, but reported elsewhere (O'Rourke, 2008). The
findings from these different research methods generally
support each other, providing more confidence in the final
conclusions. This combination of "soft" and "hard" analysis
has been used by other eminent scholars including Feldman,
Hochschild, Lane and others. A brief summary of the results
from each of the chapters is provided below.

Chapter	Results Overview
Chapter 2 – Limited Government	Deep seated beliefs about limited government exist. Response to limited government questions invokes higher levels of partisanship than other value questions. Limited government is a multidimensional concept including personal responsibility, checks and balances, federalism, opposition to special interests, mistrust of bureaucracy and individual rights. Ambivalence is caused by conflicts with equality.

Chapter 3 – Moral Traditionalism	Respondents discussed conflicts between morally traditional beliefs and freedom. Respondents showed flexibility and nuance in the application of absolute principles. Agreement on tolerance masked underlying differences in the objects of tolerance that were considered. Respondents expressed both a fear of moral decay and a concern for maintaining social freedoms. The results cast doubt on the thesis of polarization; individuals were actually divided within themselves.
Chapter 4 – Equality	Frame of reference was important for shaping beliefs about equality. Domain frame (economic, social, political) affected the expression of values. Individuals applied values differently in different domains. The choice of a social or individual frame of reference affected belief in equality. Individuals tended to believe in personal responsibility within the individual frame and equality within the social frame. Conflicts existed between different dimensions of equality, including equality before the law, equality of opportunity and equality of outcome.

Overall, this research has documented two primary sources of value ambivalence within public opinion. First, values conflict with each other. The public holds a set of deeply held core values, but it is often difficult to make these values consistent. Individuals have difficulty prioritizing their values into a value system. Second, the public often harbors both positive and negative feelings about different dimensions of the same value, or the application of values in different contexts. Ambivalence can be created when these feelings surface simultaneously.

When prioritizing values, the value of equality and limited government often conflict with each other. Policies to achieve economic and social equality are seen by many to conflict with the ideal of freedom, personal responsibility and limited government. Traditional moral beliefs are not consistently related to ideas about limited government. Some see government power as a threat to traditional morals, while others have argued for a greater intervention of government within the moral sphere. Many are concerned that government policies based on morally traditionally beliefs will limit personal freedoms.

The public's values are often multidimensional. Many are conflicted between different dimensions of limited government and equality. Even with regard to traditional moral beliefs, many have considerations both for and against traditional moral beliefs. Different interpretations of the meaning and implications of traditional moral beliefs often result in mixed feelings.

Context plays an important role in shaping values and creating ambivalence. Individuals do not apply their principles rigidly and without exception. The application of values may differ depending on the specific situations individuals find themselves in, or imagine themselves to be in. Individuals may reason differently depending on how close they are to a situation, or how closely they identify with specific groups they may think about. For equality, the group context being considered may influence the extent to which one believes in equality. Negative feelings about specific groups such as gays or Hispanics may cause some to be ambivalent towards equality. The belief in tolerance may be influenced by the specific groups that are considered as the object of tolerance.

Proximity to self may also influence the extent to which people believe in a specific value. One may believe one thing when one thinks about how a value applies to individual behavior and something different when one considers how the value may affect society at large. Whether limited government is framed within a social or an individual context may determine the extent to which this value is expressed.

Political and temporal context may also influence the expression of values. A political dialogue that links values to partisanship may serve to provide highly aware partisans cues for what they should believe. Within the context of a politically charged election, "traditional family ties" may come to have a highly political meaning. Individuals may be conflicted between logical, social, political and psychological linkages between different values and beliefs. More generally, the clear distinction between political ideas and a more abstract consideration of values is blurred for many. Partisanship may serve as the glue that ties value systems together.

Even geographical context may affect how strongly one expresses a particular value. One may compare oneself to others in a particular community to determine whether one is moderate or extreme with regard to beliefs about values such as limited government, equality or moral traditionalism. In a socially conservative rural context, one may consider themselves to be "in the middle" in their belief about limited government. Being moderate may have a different meaning for someone in a more liberal urban social context.

One conclusion that may be drawn from the importance of context to values is that the public does not have values as they have been traditionally conceived by scholars. If the value of equality, limited government or moral traditionalism may vary depending on the particular situation, one cannot be said to have a durable, unified and overarching value that affects many specific attitudes. The public's beliefs are not neatly organized around a unified and clearly delineated system of values. In short, values are not a replacement for ideology in understanding public opinion.

While values, as scholars have traditionally conceived of them, may not be clearly delineated, the public's ambivalence on specific issues does reflect deeply held beliefs. Individuals may be conflicted about their beliefs, but there are underlying cultural "values" that shape their thinking. The values of the public are nuanced and applied differently in different contexts, but they are not meaningless. They do structure individual thinking, even if they may be difficult for social scientists to build predictive models to explain them.

A related implication of the importance of context is that it can also be said to be one of the sources of value conflict. Individuals who compare their beliefs within different contexts may become aware of the inconsistencies in their beliefs and experience ambivalence. Overall, there is a lot of value conflict within individuals. This is because values are complex, influenced by context, and also because many in the public often understand that they cannot simultaneously have all of the things that they value, and they have trouble balancing these considerations.

Complexity and value conflict do not necessarily negate the importance of core values. The existence of ambivalence and value instability are not an indication of ignorance or a lack of concern for the importance of values. Rather, the public's ambivalence shows a consideration of the lines of cultural conflict that exist. A conflicted public accurately reflects the state of our politics. The fact that the public has two minds, even with regard to their core values, should not be a source of angst among scholars. It reflects both deeply felt beliefs and also provides a political resource for change for those who understand the bounds that core values set.

The findings of this study suggest new directions for future research. They show that additional cognitive interviewing can be used to help gain a better understanding of value ambivalence. The impact of geographical, political and situational context on values has not been a major theme in literature on values, and is an area worthy of additional research. More research is needed to help social scientists understand the underlying instability of the public's values, and the role that context plays in shaping response. One way to approach the study of value ambivalence is to employ branching survey questions that inject specific contextual information into the questions used to measure values. For instance, a survey could collect information on how respondents think about equality in a society-wide context as well as within an individual context. Including this type of question on an NES pilot survey would help researchers to more fully understand how the importance of context varies by different population groups, and how important it is across the population at large. More research is also needed to fully capture the impact of partisanship on the expression of values. For instance, questions could be designed to introduce partisan cues into the values questions. This might also be accomplished by varying the order of questions. Measuring the extent to which these cues change the expression of values could caste some light on whether partisanship may mold value systems.

In addition, additional information is needed to probe respondents beliefs about tolerance. Introducing group cues or other contextual information could help to provide more information on how sensitive tolerance is to the group frame of reference. Another area that is worthy of further study is how individuals place themselves on a value intensity scale. For instance, do individuals compare themselves to their friends and family, individuals in their local community, or some different reference group when deciding whether they hold a value strongly? This potential line of research could examine the role of geographical context on the expression and measurement of values. A better understanding of the frames of reference for response can help researchers understand the factors that influence value intensity, as well as factors that may alter the expression of intensity.

Appendix A: Interview Guide

Interview Goals

The purpose of the interview is to assess what the NES values questions measure. Do the NES values questions accurately measure values? Do respondents interpret these questions in different ways? What are the sources of error in the survey questions? How does the framework of values that political scientists employ match the complex structure of individual thinking about values? This interview will begin by first asking individuals to answer a selected set of NES values and other questions. Following this, the interview will probe respondents about what they think the questions mean, and why they answered the way they did.

NES Values Questions

Limited Government / Economic Individualism

Some people are afraid the government in Washington is getting too powerful for the good of the country and the individual person. Others feel that the government in Washington is not getting too strong. Do you have an opinion on this or not?

If yes, what is your feeling, do you think the government is getting too powerful or do you think the government is not getting too strong?

A. Government too powerful
B. Government not getting too strong
C. Other

Why do you think the government is too powerful \ not strong enough?

Next, I am going to ask you to choose which of two statements I read comes closer to your own opinion. You might agree to some extent with both, but we want to know which one is closer to your own views.

ONE, the less government, the better; OR TWO, there are more things that government should be doing

>   Why do you think this?

>   When you think of less government \ more government, what things do you think off?

>   Why is it that the government should \ should not do those things?

ONE, we need a strong government to handle today's complex economic problems; OR TWO, the free market can handle these problems without government being involved.

>   Why do you think this?

>   What complex economic problems do you think of?

>   Why should government \ free market handle these problems?

ONE, the main reason government has become bigger over the years is because it has gotten involved in things that people should do for themselves; OR TWO, government has become bigger because the problems we face have become bigger.

>   Why do you think this?

>   What does the phrase "government involvement in things people should do for themselves" mean to you?

>   Does the government face bigger problems? What are these?

Some people feel the government in Washington should see to it that every person has a job and a good standard of living. Suppose these people are at one end of a scale, at point 1. Others think the government should just let each person get ahead on their own.

Suppose these people are at the other end, at point 7. And, of course, some other people have opinions somewhere in between, at points 2,3,4,5, or 6. Where would you place yourself on this scale?

Why is this?

What does "seeing to it that everyone has a job and a good standard of living" mean to you?

What does a good standard of living mean to you?
What does getting ahead on your own mean to you?
Why is guaranteeing a standard of living \ getting ahead on your own more desirable?

Some people think the government should provide fewer services even in areas such as health and education in order to reduce spending. Other people feel it is important for the government to provide many more services even if it means an increase in spending. If you imagine that those who want the government to provide fewer services are at point 1 and those who want the government to provide many more services are at point 7, with others in between at points 2,3, 4, 5 and 6. Where would you place yourself on this scale.

Why is this?
Why is government spending good or bad?
What types of services would you increase \ cut?

Moral Traditionalism

Now I am going to read several statements. After each one, I would like you to tell me whether you agree strongly, agree somewhat, neither agree nor disagree, disagree, somewhat, or disagree strongly with this statement.

The world is always changing and we should adjust our view of moral behavior to those changes.

Why do you agree / disagree?

What do you think "changes in the world" refers to? What
adjustments in moral behavior do you think of?

The new lifestyles are contributing to the breakdown of our society.

Why do you agree / disagree?
What new lifestyles do you think of?
Do you think society is breaking down?
What does "breakdown of society" mean to you?

This country would have many fewer problems if there were more
emphasis on traditional family ties.

Why do you agree / disagree?
What do traditional family ties mean to you?
What kinds of problems do you think of?

We should be more tolerant of people who choose to live according
to their own moral standards, even if they are very different from our
own.

Why do you agree \ disagree?
What does more tolerant mean to you?
What kind of moral standards do you believe should \ should
not be tolerated even if you might not agree with them?

Equality

Next, I'd like to ask you about equal rights. I am going to read
several more statements. After each one, I would like you to tell me
how strongly you agree or disagree. The first statement is:

'Our society should do whatever is necessary to make sure that
everyone has an equal opportunity to succeed. 'Do you agree
strongly, agree somewhat, neither agree nor disagree, disagree
somewhat, or disagree strongly with this statement?

Why do you agree \ disagree?
What does equal opportunity mean to you?

Why should we \ should we not do whatever is necessary?
What societal actions do you think off when you hear this
statement?

'We have gone too far in pushing equal rights in this country.' (Do
you agree strongly, agree somewhat, neither agree nor disagree,
disagree somewhat, or disagree strongly with this statement?)

Why do you agree \ disagree?
What do you think this statement refers to?

'One of the big problems in this country is that we don't give
everyone an equal chance. '(Do you agree strongly, agree somewhat,
neither agree nor disagree, disagree somewhat, or disagree strongly
with this statement?)

Why do you agree \ disagree?
Why do you think \ not think this is a problem?
What does the phrase equal chance in this statement mean to
you?

'If people were treated more equally in this country we would have
many fewer problems. '(Do you agree strongly, agree somewhat,
neither agree nor disagree, disagree somewhat, or disagree strongly
with this statement?)

Why do you agree \ disagree?
What do you think of when you hear this statement?
How do you think people could be treated more equally?
What problems do you think of?

'It is not really that big a problem if some people have more of a
chance in life than others. '(Do you agree strongly, agree somewhat,
neither agree nor disagree, disagree somewhat, or disagree strongly
with this statement?)

Why do you agree \ disagree?
What do you think this statement refers to?
Why \ or why not is it a problem?

'This country would be better off if we worried less about how equal people are. '(Do you agree strongly, agree somewhat, neither agree nor disagree, disagree somewhat, or disagree strongly with this statement?)

> Why do you agree \ disagree?
> How would the country be better off? Or why wouldn't the country be better off if we worried less?

Humanitarianism

Would you say that most of the time people TRY TO BE HELPFUL, or that they are JUST LOOKING OUT FOR THEMSELVES?

> Why do you think this?
> When you think of someone trying to be helpful, what do you think off? When you think of someone looking out for themselves, what do you think off?

Do you think most people would try to TAKE ADVANTAGE of you if they got the chance or would they TRY TO BE FAIR?

> Why do you think this?
> Can you think of an example that this statement might refer too? Why do you think that people try to be fair \ take advantage when they deal with other people?

Generally speaking, would you say that MOST PEOPLE CAN BE TRUSTED, or that you CAN'T BE TOO CAREFUL in dealing with people?

> Why do you think this?
> Why do you think people can \ cannot be trusted? Can you think of an example that this question might refer too?

Would you say those people you see regularly in your neighborhood try to take advantage of others ALL OF THE TIME, MOST OF THE TIME, SOME OF THE TIME, HARDLY EVER, or NEVER?

> Why do you think this?
> Can you think of an example that this question might refer too? Why do you think that the people in your neighborhood do \ do not take advantage of others?

Would you say they treat others with respect ALL OF THE TIME, MOST OF THE TIME, SOME OF THE TIME, HARDLY EVER, or NEVER?

> Why do you think this?
> What do you think respect means in the context of this question? Can you think of an example that this statement might refer too?

Would you say that HONEST describes the people in your neighborhood EXTREMELY WELL, QUITE WELL, NOT TOO WELL, or NOT WELL AT ALL?

> Why do you think this?
> What makes you think the people in your neighborhood are honest \ not honest? Can you think of an example of this?

People have different ideas about the government in Washington. These ideas don't refer to Democrats or Republicans in particular, but just to the GOVERNMENT IN GENERAL. We want to see how you feel about these ideas. For example:

How much of the time do you think you can trust the government in Washington to do what is right--JUST ABOUT ALWAYS, MOST OF THE TIME, or ONLY SOME OF THE TIME?
> 1. JUST ABOUT ALWAYS
> 3. MOST OF THE TIME
> 5. SOME OF THE TIME
> 7. R VOL: NONE OF THE TIME

Why do you think this?
What does trust in the government mean to you?
Can you think of an example of something that enhances your trust in the government?
Can you think of something that makes you trust the government less?

Volunteer Questions

Many people say they have less time these days to do volunteer work. What about you, were you able to devote any time to volunteer work in the last 12 months or did you not do so?

Questions for the self employed

Why did you choose to become self-employed?
What do you like about being self-employed?
What do you dislike about being self-employed?
What personality traits do you need to be self-employed?
Were your parents self-employed? Are other members of your family self-employed? Are many people in your area self-employed? Do you know many people who are self-employed?
Do you think that most people would prefer to be self-employed? Why, or why not?
Do you think your status as a self-employed person influences your political beliefs or values?

Questions on school choice

Do you favor or oppose a school voucher program that would allow parents to use tax funds to send their children to the school of their choice, even if it were a private school, or haven't you thought much about this?

Why do you think this?

Do you support or oppose allowing low-income parents to use taxpayer-funded vouchers to place their kids in private or church-run schools?

Why do you think this?

If they oppose - - Would you still oppose government vouchers (so that parents can send their children to private or religious schools) if you heard that children from poorer families might not be able to attend better schools.

If they support - - Would you still favor government vouchers (so parents can send their children to private or religious schools) if you heard that it might mean less money for public schools in your area?

Demographic Information / Background Information

Can you provide me a little background about yourself?

Age
Sex
Race
Income
Education
Zip Code
Employment status – type of work / type of organization (self-employed, private, public, organization size)
Political party

Bibliography

Achen, Christopher. 1975. "Mass Political Attitudes and the Survey Response". *American Political Science Review*. Number 69: 1218-23,

Alford, Fred. 2005. *Rethinking Freedom: Why Freedom Has Lost Its Meaning and What Can Be Done to Save It*. New York: Palgrave Macmillan.

Alvarez, Michael, and John Brehm. 2002. *Hard Choices, Easy Answers*. Princeton: Princeton University Press.

Barnea, Marina, and Shalom Schwartz. 1998. "Values and Voting." *Political Psychology*. Vol. 19, No. 1

Bellah, Robert, Richard Madsen, William Sullivan, Ann Swidler, and Steven Tipton. 1996. *Habits of the Heart: Individualism and Commitment in American Life*. Berkeley: University of California Press.

Bennett, Linda, Stephan Bennett. 1990. *Living with Leviathan: Americans Coming to Terms with Big Government*. Lawrence: University Press of Kansas.

Berlin, Isaiah. 1970. *Four Essays on Liberty*. New York: Oxford Press.

Blader, Steven. 2006. "What Determines People's Fairness Judgments? Identification and Outcomes Influences Procedural Justice Evaluations Under Uncertainty." *Journal of Experimental Social Psychology*. Vol. 43: 986-994

Boaz, David. 1997. *The Libertarian Reader*. New York: The Free Press.

Campbell, Angus, Philip Converse, Warren Miller and Donald Stokes. 1960. *The American Voter*. Chicago: The University of Chicago Press.

Cantril, Albert, and Susan Cantril. 1999. *Reading Mixed Signals: Ambivalence in American Public Opinion about Government.* Washington, DC: Woodrow Wilson Center Press.

Converse, Philip. 1964. "The Nature of Belief Systems in Mass Publics." *Ideology and Discontent.* New York: The Free Press.

De Tocqueville, Alexis. 1969. *Democracy in America.* New York: Harper Perennial.

DiMaggio, Paul, John Evans, and Bethany Bryson. 1996. "Have Americans' social attitudes become more polarized?" *American Journal of Sociology.* Vol. 102, No. 3: 690-755

Elder, Glen and Rand Conger. 2000. *Children of the Land: Adversity and Success in Rural America.* Chicago: University Of Chicago Press.

Emler, Nicholas, Hammond Tarry and Angela James. 2007. "Post-Conventional Moral Reasoning and Reputation." *Journal of Research in Personality.* Vol. 41: 76-89

Emler, Nicholas; Stanley Renwick, and Barnadette Malone. 1983. "The Relationship of Moral Reasoning and Political Orientation." *Journal of Personality and Social Psychology.* Vol. 45, No. 5: 1073-1080

Ensley, Michael. 2006. "Core Values, Value Conflict, and Ideological Identification." Google Scholar.

Federico, Christopher. 2004. "When Do Welfare Attitudes Become Racialized? The Paradoxical Effects of Education". *American Journal of Political Science.* Vol. 48, No. 2: 374-391

Fee, Joan Flynn. 1981. "Symbols in Survey Questions: Solving the Problem of Multiple Word Meanings." *Political Methodology.* Vol. 7, No. 2: 71-95.

Feldman, Stanley, and Marco Steenbergen. 2001. "The Humanitarian Foundation of Public Support for Social Welfare". *American Journal of Political Science.* Vol. 45, No. 3: 658-677

Feldman, Stanley. 1988. "Structure and Consistency in Public Opinion: the role of Core Beliefs and Values. *American Journal of Political Science.* Vol. 32: 416-440

Feldman, Stanley and John Zaller. 1992. "The Political Culture of Ambivalence: Ideological Responses to the Welfare State. *American Journal of Political Science.* Vol. 36: 268-307

Feldman, Stanley. 2003. "A Conflicted Public? Equality, Fairness, and Redistribution". Prepared for presentation at the Conference on Inequality and American Democracy, Princeton University, November 7-8.

Feldman, Stanley. 1999. "Economic Values and Inequality". In *Measures of Political Attitudes*, Ed. John Robinson, Phillip Shaver, and Lawrence Wrightsman. New York: Academic Press.

Festinger, Leon. 1957. *A Theory of Cognitive Dissonance.* Palo Alto: Stanford University Press.

Fiorina, Morris, Samuel Abrams, and Jeremy Pope. 2006. *Culture War? The Myth of a Polarized America.* New York: Pearson Longman.

Fishkin, James, Kenneth Keniston and Catharine MacKinnon. 1973. "Moral Reasoning and Political Ideology." *Journal of Personality and Social Psychology.* Vol. 27, No. 1: 109-119

Fletcher, Joseph and Marie-Christine Chalmers. 1991. "Attitudes of Canadians toward Affirmative Action: Opposition, Value Pluralism, and Nonattitudes. *Political Behavior.* Vol. 13, No. 1: 67-95

Fonte, John. 2000. "Why There is a Culture War: Gramsci and Tocqueville in America." *Policy Review.* No. 104

Frank, Thomas. 2005. *What's the Matter with Kansas?* New York: Henry Holt and Company.

Free, Loyd and Hadley Cantril. 1968. *The Political Beliefs of Americans: A Study of Public Opinion.* New York: Simon and Schuster.

Friedman, Milton. 2002. *Capitalism and Freedom.* Chicago: University of Chicago Press.

Gerring, John. 1998. *Party Ideologies in America: 1828 – 1996.* New York: Cambridge University Press.

Gibbs, John. 2005. "Should Kohlberg's Cognitive Development Approach to Morality Be Replaced With a More Pragmatic Approach? Comment on Krebs and Denton." *Psychological Review.* Vol. 113, No. 3: 666-671

Gilens, Martin. 2000. *Why Americans Hate Welfare: Race, Media, and the Politics of Antipoverty Policy.* Chicago: University of Chicago Press.

Gimpel, James, Celeste Lay, Jason Schuknecht. 2003. *Cultivating Democracy: Civic Environments and Political Socialization in America.* Washington, DC: Brookings Institution Press.

Gimpel, James. 1999. *Separate Destinations: Migration, Immigration, and the Politics of Places.* University of Michigan Press.

Goren, Paul. 2004. "Party Identification and Core Values." Prepared for the 2004 Annual Meeting of the Midwest Political Science Association, April 15-18

Goren, Paul. 2000. "Political Expertise and Principled Political Thought". *Political Research Quarterly.* Vol. 53, No. 1: 117-136

Goren, Paul. 2004. "Political Sophistication and Policy Reasoning: A Reconsideration. *American Journal of Political Science.* Vol. 48, No. 3: 462-478

Goren, Paul. 2005. "Party Identification and Core Political Values." *American Journal of Political Science.* Vol. 49, No. 4: 881-896

Grant, Tobin, and Thomas Rudolph. 2003. "Value Conflict, Group Affect, and the Issue of Campaign Finance". *American Journal of Political Science.* Vol. 47, No. 3: 453-469

Green, Donald, and Jack Citrin. 1994. "Measurement Error and the Structure of Attitudes: Are Positive and Negative Judgments Opposites?" *American Journal of Political Science.* Vol. 38, No.1: 256-281

Green, Donald, Bradley Palmquist, and Eric Schickler. 2002. *Partisan Hearts & Minds.* New Haven: Yale University Press.

Hartz, Louis. 1991. *The Liberal Tradition in America.* New York: Harcourt Brace & Company.

Heise, David. 1969. "Separating Reliability and Stability in Test-Retest Correlation". *American Sociological Review.* Vol. 34, No. 1: 93-101

Hochschild, Jennifer. 1981. *What's Fair? American Beliefs about Distributive Justice.* Cambridge: Harvard University Press.

Hochschild, Jennifer. 2006. "Ambivalence About Equality in the United States or, Did Tocqueville Get it Wrong and Why Does it Matter?" *Social Justice Research.* Vol. 19, No. 1: 2006

Huckfeldt, Robert, Jeanette Mendez and Tracy Osborn. 2004. "Disagreement, Ambivalence, and Engagement: The Political Consequences of Heterogeneous. Networks". *Political Psychology.* Vol. 25 (1): 65–95

Hunter, James; Wolfe, Alan. 2006. *Is There A Culture War: A Dialogue on Values and American Public Life*. Washington D.C.: Brookings Institute Press.

Hunter, James. 1991. *Culture Wars: The Struggle to Define America*. New York: Basic Books.

Hurwitz, Jon and Mark Peffley. 1985. "A Hierarchical Model of Attitude Constraint." *American Journal of Political Science*. Vol. 29, No. 4: 871-890.

Hurwitz, Jon and Mark Peffley. 1992. "Traditional versus Social Values as Antecedents of Racial Stereotyping and Policy Conservatism. *Political Behavior*. Vol. 14, No. 4: 395-421

Inglehart, Ronald. 1985. "Aggregate Stability and Individual-Level Flux in Mass Belief System: The Levels of Analysis Paradox". *The American Political Science Review*. Vol. 79, No. 1: 97-116

Inglehart, Ronald and Paul Abramson. 1994. "Economic Security and Value Change". *The American Political Science Review*. Vol. 88, No. 2: 336-354

Jacoby, William. 1994. "Public Attitudes Toward Government Spending". *American Journal of Political Science*. Vol. 38, No. 2: 336-361

Jacoby, William. 2005. "Is it Really Ambivalence? Public Opinion Toward Government Spending" in *Ambivalence and The Structure of Political Opinion*. New York: Palgrave Macmillan.

Jacoby, William. 2000. "Issue Framing and Public Opinion on Government Spending". *American Journal of Political Science*. Vol. 44, No. 4: 750-767

Jacoby, William. 2006. "Value Choices and American Public Opinion." *American Journal of Political Science*. Vol. 50, No. 3: 706-723

Jervis, Robert. 2006. "Understanding Beliefs." *Political Psychology*. Volume 27, Issue 5: 641-663

Johnson, John, and Robert Hogan. 1981. "Moral Judgments and Self-Presentations." *Journal of Research in Personality*. Vol. 15: 57-63

Keele, Luke, Jennifer Wolak. 2006. "Value Conflict and Volatility in Party Identification". *British Journal of Political Science*. Vol. 36: 671-690

Key, V.O. 1961. *Public Opinion and American Democracy*. New York: Alfred A. Knof Publisher.

Kinder, Donald and Lynn Sanders. 1996. *Divided by Color: Racial Politics and Democratic Ideals*. Chicago: University of Chicago Press.

Kline, Rex. 2005. *Principles and Practice of Structural Equation Modeling*. New York: Guilford Press.

Kohlberg, L. 1963. "The Development of Children's Orientations Towards Moral Order. I: Sequence in the Development of Moral Thought. *Vita Humana.* Vol. 6: 11-33.

Kluegel, James, and Eliot Smith. 1986. *Beliefs About Inequality: Americans' Views of What is and What Ought to Be*. New York: Aldine Gruyter.

Koster, Willem and Jeroen Van der Waal. 2007. "Secularisation in the Netherlands: Reassessing Cultural Value Orientations and their Impact on Voting Behavior." ASSR Working Paper.

Lakoff, George. 1997. *Moral Politics: How Liberals and Conservatives Think*. Chicago: University Of Chicago Press.

Lane, Robert. 1962. *Political Ideology: Why the American Common Man Believes What He Does*. New York: The Free Press of Glencoe.

Lane, Robert. 1986. "Market Justice, Political Justice". *The American Political Science Review*. Vol.80, No. 2: 383-402

Layman, Geoffrey. 2001. *The Great Divide: Religious and Cultural Conflict in American Party Politics*. New York: Columbia University Press.

Layman, Geoffrey, and Thomas Carsey. 2002. "Party Polarization and "Conflict Extension" in the American Electorate." *American Journal of Political Science*. Vol. 46, No. 4: 786-802

Layman, Geoffrey and John Green. 2005. "Wars, Rumors of Wars: The Context of Cultural Conflict in American Political Behavior." *British Journal of Political Science*, Vol. 36.

Layman, Geoffrey. 2001. *The Great Divide: Religious and Cultural Conflict in American Party Politics*. New York: Columbia University Press.

Layman, Geoffrey, John McTague, Shanna Pearson-Merkowitz and Michael Spivey. 2007. "Which Values Divide? The Impact of Competing Parenting Visions, Culture Wars Orientations, and other Core Values on American Political Behavior. Prepared for the Annual Meeting of the Southern Political Science Association, January 4-6, 2007, New Orleans

Maddox, W. S., and S. A. Lilie. 1984. *Beyond Liberal and Conservative: Reassessing the Political Spectrum*. Washington: Cato Institute.

Martinez, Michael, Stephen Craig, and James Kane. "Pros and Cons: Ambivalence in Public Opinion." 2005. *Ambivalence and the Structure of Public Opinion*. New York: Palgrave-Macmillan.

McCann, James. 1997. "Electoral Choices and Core Value Change: The 1992 Presidential Campaign. *American Journal of Political Science*. Vol. 41, No. 2: 564-583

McClosky, Herbert; Zaller, John. 1984. *The American Ethos: Public Attitudes Toward Capitalism and Democracy*. Boston: Harvard University Press.

Meffert, Michael, Michael Guge and Milton Lodge. 2004. "Good, Bad and Ambivalent: The Consequences of Multidimensional Political Attitudes." *Studies in Public Opinion: Attitudes, Nonattitudes, Measurement Error and Change*. Princeton: Princeton University Press

Mill, John Stuart. 2000. J.S. Mill: *On Liberty and Other Writings*. Cambridge: Cambridge University Press.

Newby-Clark, I.R., Ian McGregor, and Mark Zanna. 2002. "Thinking and Caring About Cognitive Inconsistency: When and for Whom Does Attitudinal Ambivalence Feel Uncomfortable?" *Journal of Personality and Social Psychology*. Vol. 82, No. 2: 157-166

Nie, Norman, Sidney Verba, and John Petrocik. 1999. *The Changing American Voter*. New York: Excel.

Norrander, Barbara. 2000. "The Multi-Layered Impact of Public Opinion on Capital Punishment Implementation in the American States". *Political Research Quarterly*. Vol. 53, No. 4: 771-793

Norrander, Barbara and Clyde Wilcox. 2002. *Understanding Public Opinion*. Washington DC: CQ Press.

Okun, Arthur. 1975. *Equality and Efficiency: The Big Tradeoff.* Washington D.C.: Brookings Institution Press.

O'Rourke. Laurence. 2008. *Core Values: American Ambivalence Towards Equality, Limited Government and Moral Traditionalism*. Dissertation submitted to the Faculty of the Graduate School of the

University of Maryland, College Park, in partial fulfillment of the requirements for the degree of Doctor of Philosophy, 2008

Peffley, Mark and Jon Hurwitz. 1993. "Models of Attitude Constraint in Foreign Affairs" *Political Behavior*. Vol. 15, No. 1: 61-90

Peffley, Mark and Jon Hurwitz. 1985. "A Hierarchical Model of Attitude Constraint. *American Journal of Political Science,* Vol. 29, No. 4: 871-890

Pollock, Philip, Stuart Lilie, and Elliot Vittes. 1993. "Hard Issues, Core Values and Vertical Constraint: The Case of Nuclear Power". *British Journal of Political Science.* Vol. 23, No. 1: 29-50

Priester, John and Richard Petty. 1996. "The Gradual Threshold Model of Ambivalence: Relating the Positive and Negative Bases of Attitudes to Subjective Ambivalence." *Journal of Personality and Social Psychology.* Vol. 71: 431-449

Rest, James. 1975. "Longitudinal Study of the Defining Issues Test of Moral Judgment: A Strategy for Analyzing Developmental Change." *Developmental Psychology.* Vol. 11, No. 6: 738-748

Rokeach, Milton. 1974. "Change and Stability in American Value Systems, 1968-1971". *The Public Opinion Quarterly.* Vol. 38, No. 2: 222-238

Rokeach, Milton. 1973. *The Nature of Human Values.* New York: The Free Press.

Saris, Willem, and Paul Sniderman. 2004. *Studies in Public Opinion: Attitudes, Nonattitudes, Measurement Error and Change.* Princeton: Princeton University Press.

Schwartz, S. 1992. "Universals in the Content and Structure of Values: Theoretical Advances Empirical Tests in 20 Countries". In

M. Zanna (Ed.), *Advances in Experimental Social Psychology. Vol. 25*: 1-65. New York: Academic Press.

Sager, Ryan. 2006. *The Elephant in the Room: Evangelicals, Libertarians, and the Battle to Control the Republican Party.* Hoboken: John Wiley & Sons

Santorum, Rick. 2005. *It Takes a Family*. Wilmington: ISI Books.

Schuman, Howard; Presser, Stanley. 1996. *Questions & Answers in Attitude Surveys*. Thousand Oaks: Sage Publications.

Smith, Christian, Michael Emerson, Sally Gallagher, Paul Kennedy, and David Sikkink. 1997. "The Myth of Culture Wars: The Case of American Protestantism." 175-195 in *Culture Wars in American Politics: Critical Reviews of a Popular Thesis*. Rhys Williams, ed., NY: Aldine de Gruyter.

Sniderman, Paul, Richard Brody, and Phillip Tetlock. 1991. *Reasoning and Choice: Explorations in Political Psychology.* Cambridge: Cambridge University Press.

Sniderman, Paul, Richard Brody, James Kuklinski. 1984. "Policy Reasoning and Political Values: The Problem of Racial Equality." *American Journal of Political Science*. Vol. 28, No. 1: 75-94

Sparks, Paul and Kevin Durkin. 1987. "Moral Reasoning and Political Orientation: The Context Sensitivity of Individual Rights and Democratic Principles." *Journal of Personality and Social Psychology*. Vol. 52, No. 5: 931-936

Steenbergen, Marco and Paul Brewer. 2004. "The Not-So-Ambivalent Public: Policy Attitudes in the Political Culture of Ambivalence." *Studies in Public Opinion: Attitudes, Nonattitudes, Measurement Error and Change*. Princeton: Princeton University Press.

Sullivan, John, James Piereson, and George Marcus. 1979. *Tolerance and American Democracy*. Chicago: University of Chicago Press.

Taylor, S.E. 1981. "The Interface of Cognitive and Social Psychology". In J.H. Harvey (Ed.). *Cognition, Social Behavior, and the Environment*. Hillsdale, N.J.: Erlbaum.

Tetlock, Philip. 1986. "A Value Pluralism Model of Ideological Reasoning". *Journal of Personality and Social Psychology*. Vol. 50, Bo. 4: 819-827

Thomspon, Michael, Richard Ellis, and Aaron Wildavsky. 1990. *Cultural Theory*. San Francisco: Westview Press.

Tourangeau, Roger, Lance Rips, and Kenneth Rasinski. 2000. *The Psychology of Survey Response*. Cambridge: Cambridge University Press.

Wildavsky, Aaron. 1987. "Choosing Preferences by Constructing Institutions: A Cultural Theory of Preference Formation." *The American Political Science Review*. Vol. 81, No. 1: 3-22

Wiley, David and James Wiley. 1970. "The Estimation of Measurement Error in Panel Data". *American Sociological Review*. Vol. 35, No. 1: 112-117

Wilson, James Q. 1989. *The Moral Sense*. New York: Simon & Schuster.

Wolf, Alan. 1998. *One Nation, After All: What Americans Really Think About God, Country, Family, Racism, Welfare, Immigration, Homosexuality, Work, The Right, The Left and Each Other*. New York: Penguin Group.

Wuthnow, Robert. 1989. *The Struggle for America's Soul: Evangelicals, Liberals and Secularism*. Grand Rapids, MI: Eerdmans.

Yin, Robert. 2003. *Case Study Research: Design and Methods*. Thousand Oaks: Sage Publications.

Zaller, John. 1992. *The Nature and Origins of Public Opinion*. Cambridge: Cambridge University Press.

www.ingramcontent.com/pod-product-compliance
Lightning Source LLC
Chambersburg PA
CBHW051440250726
48655CB00001B/163